W9-DDA-451

Current
CONTROVERSIES

Jobs in America

Other Books in the Current Controversies Series

Current
CONTROVERSIES

Jobs in America

Debra A. Miller, Book Editor

GREENHAVEN PRESS
A part of Gale, Cengage Learning

$$(G)^0 \, 0$$

$$E, V, M = X$$

GALE
CENGAGE Learning·

Detroit • New York • San Francisco • New Haven, Conn • Waterville, Maine • London

Christine Nasso, *Publisher*
Elizabeth Des Chenes, *Managing Editor*

© 2011 Greenhaven Press, a part of Gale, Cengage Learning

Gale and Greenhaven Press are registered trademarks used herein under license.

For more information, contact:
Greenhaven Press
27500 Drake Rd.
Farmington Hills, MI 48331-3535
Or you can visit our Internet site at gale.cengage.com

For product information and technology assistance, contact us at

Gale Customer Support, 1-800-877-4253
For permission to use material from this text or product, submit all requests online at www.cengage.com/permissions

Further permissions questions can be emailed to permissionrequest@cengage.com

Articles in Greenhaven Press anthologies are often edited for length to meet page requirements. In addition, original titles of these works are changed to clearly present the main thesis and to explicitly indicate the author's opinion. Every effort is made to ensure that Greenhaven Press accurately reflects the original intent of the authors. Every effort has been made to trace the owners of copyrighted material.

Cover image copyright © Frank Huster/Aurora Photos/Corbis.

LIBRARY OF CONGRESS CATALOGING-IN-PUBLICATION DATA

Jobs in America / Debra A. Miller, book editor.
        p. cm. -- (Current controversies)
    Includes bibliographical references and index.
        ISBN 978-0-7377-5183-3 (hbk.) -- ISBN 978-0-7377-5184-0 (pbk.)
    1. Unemployment--United States--Juvenile literature. 2. Recessions--United States--Juvenile literature. 3. United States--Economic conditions--2009---Juvenile literature. I. Miller, Debra A.
        HD5724.J6874 2011
        331.13'70470973--dc22

                                                                    2010030749

Printed in the United States of America
1 2 3 4 5 6 7 14 13 12 11 10

Contents

Chapter 1: Has the Recession Caused a Jobs Crisis in America?

Yes: The Recession Has Caused a Jobs Crisis in America

or do anything but live paycheck to paycheck. The American middle class, therefore, feels financially threatened and is losing the sense of upward mobility that has traditionally defined America.

No: The Recession Has Not Caused a Jobs Crisis in America

Chapter 2: Has the Government's Economic Stimulus Package Helped to Create Jobs?

No: The Government's Economic Stimulus Package Has Not Helped to Create Jobs

Chapter 3: Will Green Jobs Solve America's Job Shortage?

As part of the upcoming push for climate legislation, many environmental groups are arguing that millions of green jobs will be created by investments in green economic recovery projects. However, conservative think tanks argue that green jobs are a myth and that climate legislation could instead cause significant harm to the U.S. economy. The truth is that it is difficult to predict the impact of a complicated government policy on a dynamic global economy.

Yes: Green Jobs Will Solve America's Job Shortage

America's growing green economy will be a great new engine for urban economic growth, innovation, and job creation. Green industries such as the solar industry are producing millions of jobs already, and the need for workers in green industries is expected to grow exponentially in coming years. America needs to prepare the next generation for this work, which will offer jobs at every skill and wage level.

The United States faces a dual challenge in its need to stimulate economic recovery and in its efforts to fight global warming. The answer to both of these challenges is the development of a clean energy economy. Making this transition will require government investment as well as private sector innovation, but this will lay a strong foundation for future economic growth and create millions of new green jobs for Americans who are out of work or who face job losses.

jobs are simply not profitable. Spain's investments in clean energy, for example, cost traditional jobs and resulted in an unemployment rate of 20 percent. Obama's green ideas, if implemented, will not save the economy but will destroy American wealth.

Chapter 4: What Should the United States Do to Create Greater Job Growth?

Foreword

By definition, controversies are "discussions of questions in which opposing opinions clash" (Webster's Twentieth Century Dictionary Unabridged). Few would deny that controversies are a pervasive part of the human condition and exist on virtually every level of human enterprise. Controversies transpire between individuals and among groups, within nations and between nations. Controversies supply the grist necessary for progress by providing challenges and challengers to the status quo. They also create atmospheres where strife and warfare can flourish. A world without controversies would be a peaceful world; but it also would be, by and large, static and prosaic.

The Series' Purpose

The purpose of the Current Controversies series is to explore many of the social, political, and economic controversies dominating the national and international scenes today. Titles selected for inclusion in the series are highly focused and specific. For example, from the larger category of criminal justice, Current Controversies deals with specific topics such as police brutality, gun control, white collar crime, and others. The debates in Current Controversies also are presented in a useful, timeless fashion. Articles and book excerpts included in each title are selected if they contribute valuable, long-range ideas to the overall debate. And wherever possible, current information is enhanced with historical documents and other relevant materials. Thus, while individual titles are current in focus, every effort is made to ensure that they will not become quickly outdated. Books in the Current Controversies series will remain important resources for librarians, teachers, and students for many years.

In addition to keeping the titles focused and specific, great care is taken in the editorial format of each book in the series. Book introductions and chapter prefaces are offered to provide background material for readers. Chapters are organized around several key questions that are answered with diverse opinions representing all points on the political spectrum. Materials in each chapter include opinions in which authors clearly disagree as well as alternative opinions in which authors may agree on a broader issue but disagree on the possible solutions. In this way, the content of each volume in Current Controversies mirrors the mosaic of opinions encountered in society. Readers will quickly realize that there are many viable answers to these complex issues. By questioning each author's conclusions, students and casual readers can begin to develop the critical thinking skills so important to evaluating opinionated material.

Current Controversies is also ideal for controlled research. Each anthology in the series is composed of primary sources taken from a wide gamut of informational categories including periodicals, newspapers, books, U.S. and foreign government documents, and the publications of private and public organizations. Readers will find factual support for reports, debates, and research papers covering all areas of important issues. In addition, an annotated table of contents, an index, a book and periodical bibliography, and a list of organizations to contact are included in each book to expedite further research.

Perhaps more than ever before in history, people are confronted with diverse and contradictory information. During the Persian Gulf War, for example, the public was not only treated to minute-to-minute coverage of the war, it was also inundated with critiques of the coverage and countless analyses of the factors motivating U.S. involvement. Being able to sort through the plethora of opinions accompanying today's major issues, and to draw one's own conclusions, can be a complicated and frustrating struggle. It is the editors' hope that Current Controversies will help readers with this struggle.

Introduction

"The severity of the current economic crisis, which some financial experts predict will linger for years, has caused many commentators to compare it to the Great Depression, while others have pointed out several significant differences between the two economic downturns."

Economists agree that the recession that hit the American economy in 2008—a crisis often called the Great Recession—has been the worst economic slowdown since the Great Depression of the 1930s. During the Great Depression, unemployment in the United States rose to 25 percent; the U.S. stock market lost more than 80 percent of its value; thousands of banks collapsed; and millions of Americans became homeless, leading to the erection of temporary shantytowns called Hoovervilles in cities across the country. Similarly, the Great Recession has brought high unemployment, a large drop in the stock market, bank failures, and millions of home foreclosures. The severity of the current economic crisis, which some financial experts predict will linger for years, has caused many commentators to compare it to the Great Depression, while others have pointed out several significant differences between the two economic downturns.

The current recession began in 2007 with a drop in housing prices, which had been steadily rising for more than a decade. The problem began with the collapse of the U.S. housing market, primarily caused by defaults of subprime loans—home loans made to buyers with very little or no verification of their income or assets. Traditionally, banks have required buyers of real estate to document their ability to pay loan payments, but subprime loans became a popular lending tool during a housing boom in which home values soared. Confident that housing values would continue to rise and that properties could be easily sold for more than their purchase prices, many subprime buyers bought homes they really could not afford by taking out adjustable rate loans with very low beginning interest rates or interest-only terms during the first few years. Often these homes were financed 100 percent, without a down payment. When housing values dropped, however, many homeowners found themselves in a situation in which they owed more on their home loans than their houses were actually worth.

As homeowners began defaulting on their loan payments, the crisis escalated. Wall Street investment banks and companies that had bought theses subprime loans, which were often deceptively packaged as low-risk mortgage securities, saw their losses mount. By the fall of 2008, the stock market had plummeted, and many large banks and other important financial institutions in the United States feared bankruptcy. Ordinary investors in the U.S. stock market watched as their portfolios dropped by half. With the banking industry in trouble, most banks stopped lending money to individuals and businesses, causing further contraction of the economy. As a result, unemployment rates skyrocketed and millions of Americans lost their jobs or homes, or both. On December 1, 2008, the National Bureau of Economic Research (NBER), a nonpartisan economic research organization that acts as the nation's economic adviser, officially declared that the country had been in a recession since December 2007. The American recession soon spread around the world to other countries that had invested in U.S. housing securities or that depended on exports to the United States.

The U.S. government responded to the growing crisis by taking several measures designed to prop up the failing banks, with the goal of encouraging banks to continue lending to boost economic growth. In 2007, the U.S. Federal Reserve, the nation's central bank in charge of regulating the money supply, cut its short-term interest rate several times and even directly bought up U.S. debt in an attempt to lower interest rates. At the same time, the George W. Bush administration and Congress negotiated an economic stimulus plan that sent out income tax rebate checks to American taxpayers. Yet the economy continued to sink despite these measures. Finally, in October 2008, President Bush supported legislation authorizing $700 billion to fund the Troubled Asset Relief Program (TARP)—a massive program aimed at rescuing failing banks. Another government effort, the Term Asset-Backed Securities Loan Facility (TALF) program, allowed the Federal Reserve to help ease credit and pressures on financial markets by purchasing mortgage-backed securities, commercial bonds of companies, and assets held by non-bank financial institutions such as credit card or auto loan companies.

The crisis was still in full swing in January 2009, when President Barack Obama took office. His administration continued to focus on the economy, working with Congress to pass another economic stimulus bill—the American Recovery and Reinvestment Act (ARRA), a $787 billion package designed to boost economic growth with a mixture of tax cuts, aid to states, and infrastructure spending. President Obama also continued the TARP and TALF programs to bail out banks and other financial institutions and backed a bailout of the U.S. auto industry and programs to guarantee loans for small businesses and provide assistance for homeowners to refinance mortgages.

Despite these actions by the federal government, high unemployment continued, reaching almost 10 percent in the fall of 2009. Other economic indicators also stayed sluggish throughout 2009 and early 2010. Altogether, the recession caused the majority of U.S. industries to cut back on production, caused a drop in household wealth larger than any since the end of World War II, and, according to the *New York Times*, caused the U.S. gross domestic product (GDP)—a measure of a country's economic output—to drop by about 1.7 percent.

Some commentators openly wondered whether the recession would deepen into a depression rivaling that of the 1930s. Most economists, however, say today's recession is simply not comparable to the Great Depression in either severity or duration. In the 1930s, for example, unemployment rates were more than twice as high as today, and the country's GDP dropped 26.5 percent—a significantly larger drop than the country has experienced since 2007. Moreover, the Great Depression lasted for close to a decade and, according to some commentators, did not lift until an economic boom was created by the onset of the Second World War. In contrast, the current recession began showing increasing signs of a turnaround much more quickly—only about two years after it started. By early 2010, unemployment rates and home foreclosures slowed; the financial industry regained profitability; and consumer spending and home sales began to rebound. Many economic experts predict that the NBER will ultimately declare that the recession had officially ended, and that the economy actually began to improve, sometime in mid-2009.

Economists and labor experts, however, are much less positive about when unemployment rates will decline to pre-recession numbers. The status of jobs in America following the 2007–2009 Great Recession is the subject of *Current Controversies: Jobs in America*. The authors of the viewpoints included in this volume present a range of opinions about issues such as whether the recession has caused a job crisis, whether the government's economic stimulus spending has helped to create jobs, whether green jobs will be the answer to the current jobs shortage, and what else can be done to generate employment growth.

CHAPTER 1

Has the Recession Caused a Jobs Crisis in America?

Chapter Preface

A lthough millions of workers in the United States suffer from unemployment, underemployment, or a lack of opportunity for advancement as a result of a deep recession in the U.S. economy, many labor experts say that young people may be the most harmed by the current economic slump. According to the U.S. Department of Labor, the unemployment rate for sixteen- to twenty-four-year-olds has risen to more than 18 percent, while the official overall unemployment rate for U.S. workers as of April 2010 was 9.7 percent. Youth unemployment is at its highest levels since the end of World War II, when the government first started keeping track of this information. Even during previous recessions, such as those in the early 1980s, 1990s, and immediately following the September 11, 2001, terrorist strike, unemployment among this age group never reached today's level. Altogether, sixteen- to twenty-four-year-olds lost 2.5 million jobs between 2007 and 2010, making them the age group hardest hit by the recession. Additionally, the underemployment rate for young people— the number of persons working part-time or less than they would like—is even worse; in mid-2009, for example, the underemployment rate for workers under age twenty-five was an astounding 31.9 percent.

Young people of color and the poor are clearly more impacted by this problem than their middle-class, white peers. According to the Bureau of Labor Statistics, African American teens between the ages of sixteen and nineteen in the fall of 2009 had an unemployment rate of 40.7 percent, while young Latinos in this age bracket were unemployed at a rate of almost 30 percent—both groups significantly worse off than white teenagers, whose unemployment rate was 23 percent. Older workers of color experience even higher rates of unemployment when compared to whites; among twenty- to twenty-four-year-olds, white workers have an unemployment rate of 13.1 percent, while African Americans in the same age range were unemployed at a rate of 27.1 percent—nearly twice as high.

The bad job market is affecting young people across the board—low-skilled high school dropouts, new college graduates, and even new lawyers and business school graduates. Even if they were able to find jobs, young people became the first to be laid off when the recession hit. Other groups affected are high school, college, or graduate school students looking for their first real jobs and finding it very difficult to start their careers. Many young people find themselves competing for entry-level positions with experienced adults, who themselves have lost jobs due to the recession. The lack of jobs and income is causing many young people to move back into their parents' homes, delaying their entry into adulthood. Worse, countless numbers of young people struggle with higher education debt as a result of rising college tuition and fees.

Some commentators have suggested that the recession may create a lost generation—a generation of young people who will suffer lifetime damage as a result of the period of joblessness hitting them so early in life. Many studies have shown that those unlucky enough to graduate during a recession or depression will feel the effects throughout their careers. They will be unable to acquire necessary job experience or be forced to work part-time in jobs that are out of their chosen fields or in positions that are beneath their abilities. As a result, these workers will face difficulty getting onto and benefiting from career ladders that otherwise might have offered them advancement and higher pay. Instead, today's young workers will have to compete with even younger workers who graduate later, as the economy improves. One study of U.S. white male college graduates, for example, found that those who graduated during the early 1980s recession earned less than workers who graduated into a better job market—even 15 years after college. Early joblessness can also have long-lasting psychological effects. Studies of Japanese workers who began their careers during Japan's 1990s recession, for example, have found that many feel depressed and stressed about their work lives, even though they are now in their thirties and established in their careers.

According to the National Association of Colleges and Employers (NACE), the job market may soon begin to improve for young college graduates. According to a NACE survey of employers conducted in December 2009, more of those polled expected to increase college hiring in 2010 than expected to decrease. This, experts say, suggests that youth unemployment may have hit bottom and could increase in coming months and years. Whether this economic recovery will materialize quickly enough and strongly enough to benefit the millions of young people struggling in today's job market remains to be seen. The authors of the viewpoints in this chapter address the issue of unemployment and whether the recession has truly created a jobs crisis in America.

The Recession Has Caused the Highest Rate of Unemployment Since the Great Depression

Don Peck

Don Peck is a writer and the deputy managing editor for the Atlantic, *an American magazine.*

How should we characterize the economic period we have now entered? After nearly two brutal years, the Great Recession appears to be over, at least technically. Yet a return to normalcy seems far off. By some measures, each recession since the 1980s has retreated more slowly than the one before it. In one sense, we never fully recovered from the last one, in 2001: the share of the civilian population with a job never returned to its previous peak before this downturn began, and incomes were stagnant throughout the decade. Still, the weakness that lingered through much of the 2000s shouldn't be confused with the trauma of the past two years, a trauma that will remain heavy for quite some time.

Joblessness and Its Effects

The unemployment rate hit 10 percent in October [2009], and there are good reasons to believe that by 2011, 2012, even 2014, it will have declined only a little. Late last year, the average duration of unemployment surpassed six months, the first time that has happened since 1948, when the Bureau of Labor Statistics began tracking that number. As of this writing, for every open job in the U.S., six people are actively looking for work.

All of these figures understate the magnitude of the jobs crisis. The broadest measure of unemployment and underemployment (which includes people who want to work but have stopped actively searching for a job, along with those who want full-time jobs but can find only part-time work) reached 17.4 percent in October, which appears to be the highest figure since the 1930s. And for large swaths of society—young adults, men, minorities—that figure was much higher (among teenagers, for instance, even the narrowest measure of unemployment stood at roughly 27 percent). One recent survey showed that 44 percent of families had experienced a job loss, a reduction in hours, or a pay cut in the past year.

This era of high joblessness will likely change the life course and character of a generation of young adults.

There is unemployment, a brief and relatively routine transitional state that results from the rise and fall of companies in any economy, and there is *unemployment*—chronic, all-consuming. The former is a necessary lubricant in any engine of economic growth. The latter is a pestilence that slowly eats away at people, families, and, if it spreads widely enough, the fabric of society. Indeed, history suggests that it is perhaps society's most noxious ill.

The worst effects of pervasive joblessness—on family, politics, society—take time to incubate, and they show themselves only slowly. But ultimately, they leave deep marks that endure long after boom times have returned. Some of these marks are just now becoming visible, and even if the economy magically and fully recovers tomorrow, new ones will continue to appear. The longer our economic slump lasts, the deeper they'll be.

If it persists much longer, this era of high joblessness will likely change the life course and character of a generation of young adults—and quite possibly those of the children behind them as well. It will leave an indelible imprint on many blue-collar white men—and on white culture. It could change the nature of modern marriage, and also cripple marriage as an institution in many communities. It may already be plunging many inner cities into a kind of despair and dysfunction not seen for decades. Ultimately, it is likely to warp our politics, our culture, and the character of our society for years.

The Long Road Ahead

Since last spring [2009], when fears of economic apocalypse began to ebb, we've been treated to an alphabet soup of predictions about the recovery. Various economists have suggested that it might look like a *V* (a strong and rapid rebound), a *U* (slower), a *W* (reflecting the possibility of a double-dip recession), or, most alarming, an *L* (no recovery in demand or jobs for years: a lost decade). This summer, with all the good letters already taken, the former labor secretary Robert Reich wrote on his blog that the recovery might actually be shaped like an *X* (the imagery is elusive, but Reich's argument was that there can be no recovery until we find an entirely new model of economic growth).

No one knows what shape the recovery will take. The economy grew at an annual rate of 2.2 percent in the third quarter of last year, the first increase since the second quarter of 2008. If economic growth continues to pick up, substantial job growth will eventually follow. But there are many reasons to doubt the durability of the economic turnaround, and the speed with which jobs will return.

Historically, financial crises have spawned long periods of economic malaise, and this crisis, so far, has been true to form. Despite the bailouts, many banks' balance sheets remain weak; more than 140 banks failed in 2009. As a result, banks have kept lending standards tight, frustrating the efforts of small businesses—which have accounted for almost half of all job losses—to invest or rehire. Exports seem unlikely to provide much of a boost; although China, India, Brazil, and some other emerging markets are growing quickly again, Europe and Japan—both major markets for U.S. exports—remain weak. And in any case, exports make up only about 13 percent of total U.S. production; even if they were to grow quickly, the impact would be muted.

Most recessions end when people start spending again, but for the foreseeable future, U.S. consumer demand is unlikely to propel strong economic growth. As of November [2009], one in seven mortgages was delinquent, up from one in 10 a year earlier. As many as one in four houses may now be underwater, and the ratio of household debt to GDP [gross domestic product], about 65 percent in the mid-1990s, is roughly 100 percent today [March 2010]. It is not merely animal spirits that are keeping people from spending freely (though those spirits are dour). Heavy debt and large losses of wealth have forced spending onto a lower path.

So what is the engine that will pull the U.S. back onto a strong growth path? That turns out to be a hard question. The *New York Times* columnist Paul Krugman, who fears a lost decade, said in a lecture at the London School of Economics [and Political Science] last summer that he has "no idea" how the economy could quickly return to strong, sustainable growth. Mark Zandi, the chief economist at Moody's Economy.com, told the Associated Press last fall, "I think the unemployment rate will be permanently higher, or at least higher for the foreseeable future. The collective psyche has changed as a result of what we've been through. And we're going to be different as a result."

One big reason that the economy stabilized last summer and fall is the stimulus; the Congressional Budget Office estimates that without the stimulus, growth would have been anywhere from 1.2 to 3.2 percentage points lower in the third quarter of 2009. The stimulus will continue to trickle into the economy for the next couple of years, but as a concentrated force, it's largely spent. Christina Romer, the chair of President [Barack] Obama's Council of Economic Advisers, said last fall, "By mid-2010, fiscal stimulus will likely be contributing little to further growth," adding that she didn't expect unemployment to fall significantly until 2011. That prediction has since been echoed, more or less, by the Federal Reserve and Goldman Sachs.

The economy now sits in a hole more than 10 million jobs deep—that's the number required to get back to 5 percent unemployment, the rate we had before the recession started, and one that's been more or less typical for a generation. And because the population is growing and new people are continually coming onto the job market, we need to produce roughly 1.5 million new jobs a year—about 125,000 a month—just to keep from sinking deeper.

Even if the economy were to immediately begin producing 600,000 jobs a month—more than double the pace of the mid-to-late 1990s, when job growth was strong—it would take roughly two years to dig ourselves out of the hole we're in. The economy could add jobs that fast, or even faster—job growth is theoretically limited only by labor supply, and a lot more labor is sitting idle today than usual. But the U.S. hasn't seen that pace of sustained employment growth in more than 30 years. And given the particulars of this recession, matching idle workers with new jobs—even once economic growth picks up—seems likely to be a particularly slow and challenging process.

The construction and finance industries, bloated by a decade-long housing bubble, are unlikely to regain their former share of the economy, and as a result many out-of-work finance professionals and construction workers won't be able to simply pick up where they left off when growth returns—they'll need to retrain and find new careers. (For different reasons, the same might be said of many media professionals and autoworkers.) And even within industries that are likely to bounce back smartly, temporary layoffs have generally given way to the permanent elimination of jobs, the result of workplace restructuring. Manufacturing jobs have of course been moving overseas for decades, and still are; but recently, the outsourcing of much white-collar work has become possible. Companies that have cut domestic payrolls to the bone in this recession may choose to rebuild them in Shanghai, Guangzhou, or Bangalore, accelerating offshoring decisions that otherwise might have occurred over many years.

Starting Over

New jobs will come open in the U.S. But many will have different skill requirements than the old ones. "In a sense," says Gary Burtless, a labor economist at the Brookings Institution, "every time someone's laid off now, they need to start all over. They don't even know what industry they'll be in next." And as a spell of unemployment lengthens, skills erode and behavior tends to change, leaving some people unqualified even for work they once did well.

Ultimately, innovation is what allows an economy to grow quickly and create new jobs as old ones obsolesce and disappear. Typically, one salutary side effect of recessions is that they eventually spur booms in innovation. Some laid-off employees become entrepreneurs, working on ideas that have been ignored by corporate bureaucracies, while sclerotic firms in declining industries fail, making way for nimbler enterprises. But according to the economist Edmund Phelps, the innovative potential of the U.S. economy looks limited today. In a recent *Harvard Business Review* article, he and his co-author, Leo Tilman, argue that dynamism in the U.S. has actually been in decline for a decade; with the housing bubble fueling easy (but unsustainable) growth for much of that time, we just didn't notice. Phelps and Tilman finger several culprits: a patent system that's become stifling; an increasingly myopic focus among public companies on quarterly results, rather than long-term value creation; and, not least, a financial industry that for a generation has focused its talent and resources not on funding business innovation, but on proprietary trading, regulatory arbitrage, and arcane financial engineering. None of these problems is likely to disappear quickly. Phelps, who won a Nobel Prize for his work on the "natural" rate of unemployment, believes that until they do disappear, the new floor for unemployment is likely to be between 6.5 percent and 7.5 percent, even once "recovery" is complete.

It's likely, then, that for the next several years or more, the job environment will more closely resemble today's environment than that of 2006 or 2007—or for that matter, the environment to which we were accustomed for a generation. Heidi Shierholz, an economist at the Economic Policy Institute, notes that if the recovery follows the same basic path as the last two (in 1991 and 2001), unemployment will stand at roughly 8 percent in 2014.

"We haven't seen anything like this before: a really deep recession combined with a really extended period, maybe as much as eight years, all told, of highly elevated unemployment," Shierholz told me. "We're about to see a big national experiment on stress."

The Recession Will Result in Several Years of Joblessness

Josh Bivens and Heidi Shierholz

Josh Bivens and Heidi Shierholz are economists with the Economic Policy Institute, a Washington-based think tank that focuses on the economic condition of low- and middle-income Americans.

The National Bureau of Economic Research (NBER), the nation's arbiter for dating business cycles, is apt to conclude that the recession officially ended in the middle of 2009. Yet consistent job growth has yet to arrive and the unemployment rate will probably not peak until the second half of this year [2010]. In short, this recovery is currently "jobless" and has been for quite some time. Worse, even when it is no longer technically jobless (that is, when we have positive employment growth), the unemployment rate will likely not fall substantially for a year or even longer.

Defining Recovery

To many, a jobless recovery and rising unemployment rates occurring simultaneously as jobs return seems contradictory—what is recovery, after all, if not a return to economic security? The simplest (though unsatisfying) answer is that the NBER mostly bases its official end-date of recessions on when output (goods and services) growth, not employment growth, resumes. This [viewpoint] examines the reasons why recovery in *employment* has lagged far behind recovery of output in recent recessions, and explains why it is quite likely that this long lag between output and employment growth (absent strong policy interventions aimed at spurring them) will hap-

Josh Bivens and Heidi Shierholz, "For Job Seekers, No Recovery in Sight—Why Prospects for Job Growth and Unemployment Remain Dim," Economic Policy Institute, March 31, 2010. Reproduced by permission.

pen again. It predicts that it will be many years before the labor market is even as healthy as it was in December 2007.

The U.S. economy has lost 8.4 million jobs since the recession began, while it should have added 2.7 million jobs simply to keep up with population growth.

The U.S. economy has lost 8.4 million jobs since the recession began, while it should have added 2.7 million jobs simply to keep up with population growth. This means the labor market is now roughly 11.1 million jobs below what would be needed to restore the pre-recession unemployment rate. The main findings of the [viewpoint] are:

- Jobless recoveries happen when growth in gross domestic product (GDP) [a measure of total economic output] is too slow relative to the growth of productivity and average hours worked per employee to create jobs.

- Measured productivity growth often accelerates in the early phase of business cycle recoveries and this reflects the ability of firms to accommodate rising demand for their output without resorting to hiring. How long firms make this accommodation will be a key determinant of how long the current recovery remains jobless.

- The current recession has been characterized by an even larger fall in total hours worked than in jobs. If employers restore hours for existing employees before hiring new workers, this will result in a longer jobless recovery.

- The unemployment rate can rise even if job growth returns, as those who exited the labor force (and are therefore not counted among the unemployed) during the recession begin to search for jobs once again.

- The best cure for a jobless recovery is straightforward: faster GDP growth.

- The way to implement this cure is to take aggressive action to spur job creation through greater federal spending, transfer payments, and temporary tax credits for firms that expand employment. While the deficit increase needed to spur job creation imposes no significant *economic* constraint on boosting GDP growth, if *political* considerations constrain measures to boost GDP growth, then policy makers should seek to maximize both the *labor-intensity* of given GDP increase (that is, how many total hours of employment growth are associated with a given GDP increase) as well as the *job-intensity* (that is, how many jobs are associated with a given increase in total hours). Among policies to boost the labor and job intensity of GDP growth are tax credits to firms to either add to payroll or shorten the work week.

Jobless Recoveries: A New Phase in American Business Cycle?

The excruciatingly long lag time between recovery in some measures of economic performance like GDP and recovery in most Americans' job-market prospects following recessions is a relatively modern phenomenon. After the seven recessions that occurred between 1948 and 1980, the average lag time between the official end of the recession and the return to pre-recession levels of employment was a little over nine months and never took more than a year. . . .

The 1980s recession followed the pattern that prevailed between 1948 and 1980, when the pre-recession employment peak was reached 11 months after the official end of the recession.

However, for the next two recessions (beginning in 1990 and 2001), the lag time was much longer. Following the 1990 recession it took 23 months to reach the pre-recession peak; following the 2001 recession it took 39 months. . . .

The most hopeful scenario, with employment rising at the rate that characterized the 1980s recession, would see employment regaining its pre-recession peak by September 2011 if this employment growth started in February 2010 (which is an optimistic assumption). If employment grew at the rate characterizing the 1990s and 2000s employment recoveries, this December 2007 peak would be regained in May 2013 and November 2014, respectively.

Will job-market prospects recover relatively quickly following the end of the 2008 recession, as they did in the first eight business cycles of the post–World War II era, or will they continue the pattern established in the two most recent business cycles and remain poor for years after the official economic recovery is under way? The next section takes up this question.

The Arithmetic of Jobless Recoveries: Back to the 1980s, '90s, or 2000s?

To understand how jobless recoveries happen, one must understand the relationships between GDP growth, productivity, hours per worker, and employment. Simply put, GDP is the product of multiplying total employment, productivity (defined as output per hour worked in the economy), and average hours worked per employee. . . .

A standard approximation of employment *growth* then just becomes the growth rate of GDP minus the sum of the growth rates of productivity and average hours. . . .

From here, it is easy to see that employment growth can be negative (or flat) even if GDP growth is positive—so long as the sum of growth rates of productivity and average hours rise faster than GDP growth, *employment* will shrink even as *total economic output* (GDP) rises. . . .

In the 1980s recovery, GDP growth was fast enough to outpace the sum of productivity and average hours growth and lead to rapid employment gains. In the 1990s and 2000s this was not the case. This, in a nutshell, is why we had jobless recoveries in the latter two business cycles. . . .

Productivity growth tends to surge in the early phases of recovery and dampen employment growth—and this is true in each of the last three recoveries.

Some highlights (or lowlights for job creation) are discussed in some detail below, but can be roughly summarized as:

- First, a key feature of the early stage of each recovery was an acceleration of measured productivity growth. In the long run, productivity growth is an unalloyed boon—being able to produce more output with a given workforce is the source of rising living standards. However, rising measured productivity growth in the early stage of a recovery is a sign that firms are able to accommodate rising demands for their output without hiring. Hence, how much measured productivity growth surges in the early stages of recovery from the 2008 recession will determine how easily GDP growth translates into job growth. Given this uncertainty about how much productivity growth can allow firms to absorb output growth without hiring, the lesson seems clear: strong output growth is needed for strong employment growth, period.

- Second, besides the substantial gap facing the economy from the 8.4 million jobs actually lost since the recession began, another gap is the large reduction in *average hours worked per week* during the recession. If employers can accommodate growing demand for their firms' output by increasing average hours of their existing workforce rather than adding new employees in the early stages of recovery, this will also provide a powerful drag on job growth.

How Long Can Firms Boost Output Without Hiring?

As noted above, productivity growth tends to surge in the early phases of recovery and dampen employment growth—and this is true in each of the last three recoveries. If one supposes that the recession beginning in 2008 actually ended in June 2009 (this is probably close to where the recession will eventually be officially declared having ended), then productivity growth in the first two quarters of the recovery has averaged a staggeringly high 7.4% annualized growth rate. These productivity growth rates are implausibly high and may well be revised slightly downwards. Yet, evidence from the last half of 2009 suggests that the typical early-recovery spike in productivity seems poised to repeat and may even accelerate faster than usual. If this productivity spike occurs, it would follow a recession that did not experience much of a slowdown in productivity growth relative to the expansion years immediately preceding it. In this sense, the current business cycle is looking very similar to that of the early 2000s.

For decades productivity growth in the U.S. economy was generally thought to be pro-cyclical—meaning that productivity fell during recessions and rose during periods of tight labor markets. This meant productivity trends somewhat dampened the negative relationship between employment and output growth over business cycles. As productivity fell just as demand output fell (i.e., during recessions), this meant that firms did not need to lay off as many workers to cope with the downturn.

A common interpretation of this pro-cyclical behavior of productivity growth was that firms engaged in "labor-hoarding" during recessions—keeping on workers even if there was not enough current output demanded from them to fully use the workers. This labor-hoarding was often thought to reflect that employers "valued the match" they had made with their employees, calculating that shedding workers during a recession and then rehiring during expansion imposed costs hefty enough to justify the labor-hoarding during bad times. Evidence of labor-hoarding in the recession can be found in the negative productivity growth rates that characterize the recessions beginning in the 1980s and 1990s. This labor-hoarding does not seem to be a feature of more recent business cycles, as productivity growth remains strong (even relative to long-run trends) over the entire recessions that started in 2001 and 2008.

Even worse, the relatively strong productivity growth of the 2001 recession was still followed by a modest acceleration of this growth in the first two years of recovery. In a sense, employment changes were not muffled at all during the recession from decelerating productivity, yet they were muffled during the initial stages of recovery, as firms were able to accommodate output growth without hiring. This unfortunate pattern seems poised to repeat: Productivity growth has held up well throughout the recession beginning in 2008 and began accelerating in the last half of 2009. . . .

How Bad Is the Drop in Hours?

Further, the very large employment declines we have seen during this recession have actually been muted by the fact that average hours per employee have also fallen.

Since December 2007, while private-sector jobs are down 7.4%, total private-sector hours are down 9.5%, or almost 30% more. As GDP continues growing as it has in the past two quarters, some of the employment gains that might accompany this output growth will instead be absorbed by rising average hours per employee, as employers restore the hours of their existing employees before hiring new workers. The scope of this issue is perhaps surprisingly large—to simply restore average hours from their current level (33.9 hours per week) to their pre-recession level (34.7 hours per week) at the current level of employment would be equivalent to adding 2.5 million new jobs.

With the high productivity growth rate so far in this recession and (possibly) recovery, the large gap left from the sharp decline in average weekly hours worked, and the relatively low projections by most professional forecasters for GDP growth in 2010, we seem certain to continue with consistent output growth, but no real change in the huge jobs hole left by the recession. . . .

The Need for Action

Jobless recoveries are easy to explain arithmetically—they happen when GDP does not rise fast enough to overcome the job-killing effects of productivity growth and rising average hours. What economic forces cause each of these variables to take the specific path that they do in any given time period, however, is much harder to pin down analytically.

Though we cannot precisely forecast how these economic variables will behave, we are not helpless in the face of a looming jobless recovery. Policy makers can take steps to boost GDP growth, slow the rate of productivity growth, and/or shorten average hours worked per week in the short term, all of which will add to job creation. Given the importance of the labor market's health to the living standards of working- and middle-class Americans, and given the dire outlook for this health in coming years, policy makers should start taking these steps immediately.

The Recession Is Destroying the American Middle Class

Judy Isikow

Judy Isikow is an award-winning producer for ABC News.

The American middle class, long the backbone of this country and the envy of the rest of the world, is dispirited. It is feeling financially threatened and may be in danger of losing its sense of upward mobility, the mojo that underpins the U.S. economy and America's famously optimistic attitude.

A new ABC News poll shows that while nearly 50 percent of Americans see themselves as middle class, four in 10 say they're struggling to hold on.

A Struggling American Middle Class

The numbers give a sense of Americans feeling stalled. Only 6 percent of those in the middle class see themselves moving up beyond their current status, according to the poll results.

In the last 20 years, family income has increased by only 20 percent, according to the U.S. Census Bureau compared to almost 100 percent growth in the 30 years prior. Meanwhile the cost of basic needs like housing and health insurance have continued to rise. . . .

Those grinding numbers threaten to replace the country's sunny outlook with a sense of unease and it could redefine the middle class.

Harvard University law professor Elizabeth Warren has studied the American middle class for 20 years. She says the designation of middle class has been more a state of mind than a tax bracket. It comes down to people's actions, and she believes those actions are what makes this country great.

Judy Isikow, "Defining the American Middle Class in Recession," abcnews.go.com, March 16, 2010. Reproduced by permission.

"Middle-class people are people who mow the lawn, who pick up litter on the streets. They go to PTA meetings and invest not just in themselves, but in their children and communities," she says.

"It's about aspiration, it's about how we see our family and what hopes we have for our children that's middle class," added Warren, who is also chair of the Congressional Oversight Panel.

"It's the work done by the middle class, it's the consumption of the middle class that keeps the economy turning," she says.

But now, Warren says, "Millions of Americans and families are living one pink slip, one bad diagnosis away from complete economic collapse."

Recession Effects

Since the recession began more than 5.2 million Americans have lost their homes in the financial crisis, according to Moody's Economy.com [a financial research firm].

Ten years ago, health insurance cost American families $979.1 billion, per year. Today America is spending $1.88 trillion dollars, according to *Health Affairs*, a leading journal of health policy in the United States.

And when it comes to planning for the future, 33 percent of American families say they have decreased the amount they are saving for college, while 15 percent say they are not saving at all, according to a Sallie Mae/Gallup poll.

Millions of jobs have been lost and millions more homes are underwater. . . . Bad economic news has hit middle-class families hard.

"They've seen their own lives as stretched and strained, and barely able to make it from month to month. And then they look at the lives their children will have; they recognize their children must have a college education to make it in the middle class, and yet the cost of college rises as the family's ability to save keeps going down," said Warren.

The same trend is being seen when it comes to saving for retirement. A study done by Employee Benefit Research Institute found that only 69 percent of American workers now say they save anything for retirement. And the amount they are saving continues to shrink. Americans now save just one penny for every dollar earned, according to Matthew Slaughter at the Tuck School of Business at Dartmouth.

That's where the roads in America today seem to diverge. Millions of jobs have been lost and millions more homes are underwater, with 25 percent of their value lost, on average. All that bad economic news has hit middle-class families hard, even as the banks that caused the financial crisis took $204 billion in bailout money to generate $6 billion in profits in just 3 months.

Warren's Oversight Panel, the group in charge of overseeing and examining the financial bailout, says it's time for the banks to demonstrate that we're all in this together in America. If not, consumers will have to find their way out on their own.

"The notion of a solid middle class that can withstand some really hard blows, it's just not there anymore. If we lose the middle class, we are a different country," Warren said. "I don't know what country that is, but it's a country with a large, rich population and then just a long, gray line of people who are constantly turning over, living job to job, paycheck to paycheck, illness to illness, moving up and down that line."

That country, she says, is not America.

The Recession Is a Catastrophe for African Americans

Arlene Holt Baker

Arlene Holt Baker is the executive vice president of the American Federation of Labor and Congress of Industrial Organizations (AFL-CIO), a large federation of American unions.

More than 16 percent of African Americans are officially unemployed. Creating more jobs is a matter of survival.

America's jobs crisis is hurting everyone. But for African American communities, it's a catastrophe. Unless America takes immediate steps to create jobs now—jobs where the people are—the damage will become even more entrenched, threatening generations of African Americans.

The Plight of African American Communities

So many of the communities we live in were in economic free fall before this recession even started. The demise of manufacturing and construction jobs robbed millions of us entry to the middle class and plunged African American communities into economic tatters. More than 16 percent of African Americans are officially unemployed—and that's not counting those who can only find part-time jobs or have just given up looking for work altogether.

Unemployment has shrunk local tax bases, eroding education and destroying public jobs, public services, public safety and, in general, the quality of life in our communities. In the metropolitan areas with the nation's highest unemployment rates, most of the residents are black. And the places where

Arlene Holt Baker, "Create Jobs Where the People Are," *The Root*, January 17, 2010. Reprinted with permission of the author.

blacks live were deliberately targeted for subprime lending schemes—so we've been disproportionately slammed by foreclosures and bankruptcies.

This is no ordinary recession. The fabric of whole communities has been unraveled. The economic scarring of African Americans may endure for generations. The child who is hungry today and can't concentrate in her overcrowded classroom starts with the deck stacked against her. Maybe her state has cut teachers, guidance counselors, police and funding for higher education. Twenty to 30 percent of the adults around her may be unemployed. Her pain is not hers alone—with so little opportunity, her pain will also be her children's.

Unlike the era of the Great Migration northward in search of jobs and hope, today there's nowhere left for us to go. So we need to create jobs where the people who need them are.

Immediate Action Needed

The AFL-CIO [American Federation of Labor and Congress of Industrial Organizations] has laid out a five-point plan to save and create millions of jobs in the next year. Nowhere is immediate action more needed than among the African American community, who has been carrying the heaviest weight of the crisis.

First, Congress must extend for at least 12 months the lifeline of unemployment insurance, health care and food assistance for workers who have lost jobs. A record 38 percent of the unemployed overall has been without jobs for 27 weeks or more, but African Americans remain jobless for an average of five weeks longer than others. Maintaining the lifeline is not an option—it's food on the table and a roof overhead. In short, it's survival.

We've also got to put people to work fixing America's broken infrastructure—our crumbling schools and bridges, highways and water and sewer systems. At the same time we can pump life back into deindustrialized communities by retooling shuttered factories and building new facilities for jobs in green technologies. It's happening now in places like Gary, [Indiana], and Detroit—but Congress has to invest more to jump-start these efforts and take them to a far larger scale. Restore middle-class jobs and we restore hope.

We need to rescue states and communities that are being strangled by budget shortfalls. Not only can federal investments save desperately needed middle-class jobs, they can make distressed communities safer and much more livable. The economic recovery package passed earlier this year helped, but it didn't approach the level of need.

Small businesses are the key engine for local job growth— but the banks we so generously bailed out still aren't lending. Congress can change that by hiring community banks to lend leftover TARP [Troubled Asset Relief Program, a federal bank bailout program] money directly to small and medium-sized businesses for job creation right where we live.

One of the most significant things we can do for jobless African Americans and distressed communities is to connect people without work directly to work that is crying to be done—from cleaning up abandoned buildings to driving seniors to the grocery store. If the private sector won't create jobs, government must. These cannot take the place of existing public jobs and must pay competitive wages so we're not replacing good state and local government jobs with temporary or poorly paid positions.

Saving and creating jobs alone won't solve the engrained economic problems of African Americans in devastated communities. But it's the start we need—right now—as we continue rebuilding an economy that works for *our* streets, not just Wall Street.

Corporate Monopolies, Not Recessions, Are to Blame for the Lack of Jobs in America

Barry C. Lynn and Phillip Longman

Barry C. Lynn is the director of the Markets, Enterprise and Resiliency Initiative and a senior fellow in the Economic Growth Program at the New America Foundation, a public policy institute. Phillip Longman is a senior research fellow at the New America Foundation, currently concentrating on health care policy, including delivery system reform and environmental and nutritional factors affecting public health.

If any single number captures the state of the American economy over the last decade, it is zero. That was the net gain in jobs between 1999 and 2009—nada, nil, zip. By painful contrast, from the 1940s through the 1990s, recessions came and went, but no decade ended without at least a 20 percent increase in the number of jobs.

Reasons for Weak Job Creation

Many people blame the great real estate bubble of recent years. The idea here is that once a bubble pops it can destroy more real-world business activity—and jobs—than it creates as it expands. There is some truth to this. But it doesn't explain why, even when the real estate bubble was at its most inflated, so few jobs were created compared to the tech-stock bubble of the late '90s. Between 2000 and 2007 American businesses created only seven million jobs, before the great recession destroyed more than that. In the '90s prior to the dot-com bust, they created more than twenty-two million jobs.

Barry C. Lynn and Phillip Longman, "Who Broke America's Jobs Machine? Why Creeping Consolidation Is Crushing American Livelihoods," *The Washington Monthly*, March–April 2010. Reproduced by permission.

Others point to the diffusion of new technologies that reduce the number of workers needed to produce and sell manufactured products like cars and services like airline reserva-
tions. But throughout economic history, even as new
technologies like the assembly line and the personal computer
destroyed large numbers of jobs, they also empowered people
to create new and different ones, often in greater numbers. Yet
others blame foreign competition and offshoring, and point to
all the jobs lost to China, India, or Mexico. Here, too, there is
some truth. But U.S. governments have been liberalizing our
trade laws for decades; although this has radically changed the
type of jobs available to American workers—shifting vast
chunks of the U.S. manufacturing sector overseas, for instance—there is little evidence that this has resulted in any
lasting decline in the number of jobs in America.

---

*One of the more compelling potential explanations [for
what killed the great American jobs machine] has been
conspicuously absent from the national conversation:
monopolization.*

Moreover, recent Labor Department statistics show that
the loss of jobs here at home, be it the result of sudden economic crashes or technological progress or trade liberaliza-
tion, does not appear to be our main problem at all. Though
few people realize it, the rate of job destruction in the private
sector is now 20 percent lower than it was in the late '90s,
when managers at America's corporations embraced outsourcing and downsizing with an often manic intensity. Rather, the
lack of net job growth over the last decade is due mainly to
the creation of fewer new jobs. As recent Labor Department
statistics show, even during the peak years of the housing

boom, job creation by existing businesses was 14 percent lower than it was in the late '90s.

The problem of weak job creation certainly can't be due to increased business taxes and regulation, since both were slashed during the Bush years. Nor can the explanation be insufficient consumer demand; throughout most of the last decade, consumers and the federal government engaged in a consumption binge of world-historical proportions.

Other, more plausible explanations have been floated for why the rate of job creation seems to have fallen. One is that the federal government made too few investments in the 1980s and '90s in things like basic R&D [research and development] so the pipeline of technological innovation on which new jobs depend began to run dry in the 2000s. Another is that a basic shift in competitiveness has taken place—that countries like India, with educated but relatively low-cost workforces, have become more natural homes for jobs-producing sectors like IT [information technology].

Evidence is growing . . . that the radical, wide-ranging consolidation of recent years has reduced job creation at both big and small firms simultaneously.

But while the mystery of what killed the great American jobs machine has yielded no shortage of debatable answers, one of the more compelling potential explanations has been conspicuously absent from the national conversation: monopolization. The word itself feels anachronistic, a relic from the age of the Rockefellers and Carnegies [wealthy, powerful American families]. But the fact that the term has faded from our daily discourse doesn't mean the thing itself has vanished—in fact, the opposite is true. In nearly every sector of our economy, far fewer firms control far greater shares of their markets than they did a generation ago.

Impact of Legislation and Industry

Indeed, in the years after officials in the [Ronald] Reagan administration radically altered how our government enforces our antimonopoly laws, the American economy underwent a truly revolutionary restructuring. Four great waves of mergers and acquisitions—in the mid-1980s, early '90s, late '90s, and between 2003 and 2007—transformed America's industrial landscape at least as much as globalization. Over the same two decades, meanwhile, the spread of mega-retailers like Wal-Mart and Home Depot and agricultural behemoths like Smithfield and Tyson resulted in a more piecemeal approach to consolidation, through the destruction or displacement of countless independent family-owned businesses.

It is now widely accepted among scholars that small businesses are responsible for most of the net job creation in the United States. It is also widely agreed that small businesses tend to be more inventive, producing more patents per employee, for example, than do larger firms. Less well established is what role concentration plays in suppressing new business formation and the expansion of existing businesses, along with the jobs and innovation that go with such growth. Evidence is growing, however, that the radical, wide-ranging consolidation of recent years has reduced job creation at both big and small firms simultaneously. At one extreme, ever more dominant Goliaths increasingly lack any real incentive to create new jobs; after all, many can increase their earnings merely by using their power to charge customers more or pay suppliers less. At the other extreme, the people who run our small enterprises enjoy fewer opportunities than in the past to grow their businesses. The Goliaths of today are so big and so adept at protecting their turf that they leave few niches open to exploit.

Over the next few years, we can use our government to do many things to promote the creation of new and better jobs in America. But even the most aggressive stimulus packages and tax cutting will do little to restore the sort of open market competition that, over the years, has proven to be such an important impetus to the creation of wealth, well-being, and work. Consolidation is certainly not the only factor at play. But any policy maker who is really serious about creating new jobs in America would be unwise to continue to ignore our new monopolies.

It's not as if Americans are entirely unaware of how consolidated our economic landscape is, or that this is a perilous way to do business. The financial crisis taught us how dangerously concentrated our financial sector has become, particularly since Washington responded to the near-catastrophic collapse of banks deemed "too big to fail" by making them even bigger. Today, America's five largest banks control a stunning 48 percent of bank assets, double their share in 2000 (and that's actually one of the *less* consolidated sectors of our economy). Similarly, the debate over health insurance reform awakened many of us to the fact that, in many communities across America, insurance companies enjoy what amounts to monopoly power. Some of us are aware, too, through documentaries like *Food, Inc.*, of how concentrated agribusiness and food processing have become, and of the problems with food quality and safety that can result.

Even so, most Americans still believe that our economy remains the most wide open, competitive, and vibrant market system the world has ever seen. Unfortunately, the stories we have told ourselves about competition in America over the past quarter century are simply no longer true.

Examples of Monopolization

Perhaps the easiest way to understand this is to take a quick walk around a typical grocery or big-box store, and look more closely at what has taken place in these citadels of consumer choice in the generation since we stopped enforcing our antitrust laws.

The first proof is found in the store itself. If you are stocking up on basic goods, there's a good chance you are wandering the aisles of a Wal-Mart. After all, the company is legendarily dominant in retail, controlling, for instance, 25 percent of groceries sales in some states and 40 percent of DVD sales nationwide.

But at least the plethora of different brands vying for your attention on the store shelves suggests a healthy, competitive marketplace, right? Well, let's take a closer look.

In the health aisle, the vast array of toothpaste options on display is mostly the work of two companies: Colgate-Palmolive and Procter & Gamble, which split nearly 70 percent of the U.S. market and control even such seemingly independent brands as Tom's of Maine. And in many stores the competition between most brands is mostly choreographed anyway. Under a system known as "category management," retailers like Wal-Mart and their largest suppliers openly cooperate in determining everything from price to product placement.

Over in the cold case we find an even greater array of beer options, designed to satisfy almost any taste. We can choose among the old standbys like Budweiser, Coors, and Miller Lite. Or from a cornucopia of smaller brands, imports and specialty brews like Stella Artois, Redbridge, Rolling Rock, Beck's, Blue Moon, and Stone Mill Pale Ale. But all these brands—indeed more than 80 percent of all beers in America—are controlled by two companies, Anheuser-Busch InBev and MillerCoors.

Need milk? In many parts of the country, the choices you see in the Wal-Mart dairy section are almost entirely an illusion. In many stores, for instance, you can pick among jugs labeled with the names PET Dairy, Mayfield, or Horizon. But don't waste too much time deciding: All three brands are owned by Dean Foods, the nation's largest dairy processor, and Wal-Mart's own Great Value brand containers are sometimes filled by Dean as well. Indeed, around 70 percent of milk sold in New England—and up to 80 percent of milk peddled in some other parts of the country—comes from Dean plants. Besides dominating the retail dairy market, Dean has been accused of collaborating with Dairy Farmers of America, another giant company that buys milk from independent farmers and provides it to Dean for processing and distribution, to drive down the price farmers are paid while inflating its own profits.

The food on offer outside of the refrigerator aisle isn't much better. The boxes on the shelves are largely filled with the corn-derived products that are the basic building block of most modern processed food; about 80 percent of all the corn seed in America and 95 percent of soybean seeds contain patented genes produced by a single company: Monsanto. And things are just as bad farther down the ingredients list—take an additive like ascorbic acid (vitamin C), produced by a Chinese cartel that holds more than 85 percent of the U.S. market.

How about pet food? There sure seems to be a bewildering array of options. But if you paid close attention to coverage of the massive pet food recall of 2007, you will remember that five of the top six independent brands—including those marketed by Colgate-Palmolive, Mars, and Procter & Gamble—relied on a single contract manufacturer, Menu Foods, as did seventeen of the top twenty food retailers in the United States that sell "private label" wet pet foods under their store brands, including Safeway, Kroger, and Wal-Mart. The Menu Foods recall covered products that had been retailed under a phenomenal 150 different product names.

Heading out to the parking lot should give us some respite from all of this—surely the vehicles here reflect a last bastion of American-style competition, no? After all, more than a dozen big carmakers sell hundreds of different models in America. But it's a funny kind of competition, one that's not nearly as competitive as it looks. To begin with, more than two-thirds of the iron ore used to make the steel in all those cars is likely provided by just three firms (two of which are trying to merge). And it doesn't stop there. A decade ago, all the big carmakers were for the most part vertically integrated, and they kept their supply systems largely separate from one another. Today, however, the outsourcing revolution, combined with monopolization within the supply base, means the big companies increasingly rely on the same outside suppliers—even the same factories—for components like piston rings and windshield wiper blades and door handles. Ever wonder why Toyota came out so strongly in favor of a bailout for General Motors last year [2009]? One reason is they knew if that giant fell suddenly, it would knock over many of the suppliers that they themselves—as well as Nissan and Honda—depend on to make their own cars.

And don't fool yourself that this process of monopolization affects only America's working classes. What's happened to down-market retail has happened to department stores as well. Think Macy's competes with Bloomingdale's? Think again. Both are units of a holding company called Macy's Inc., which, under its old name, Federated [Department Stores Inc.], spent the last two decades rolling up control of such department store brand names as Marshall Field's, Hecht's, Broadway, and Bon Marché. A generation ago, even most midsized cities in America could boast of multiple independent department stores. Today a single company controls roughly 800 outlets, in a chain that stretches from the Atlantic to the Pacific.

Monopolization Destroys Jobs and Inhibits Job Creation

In school, many of us learned that the greatest dangers posed by monopolization are political in nature—namely, consolidation of power in the hands of the few and the destruction of the property and liberty of individual citizens. Most of us probably also learned in seventh-grade civics class how firms with monopoly power can gouge consumers by jacking up prices. (And indeed they often do; a recent study of mergers found that in four out of five cases, the merged firms increased prices on products ranging from Quaker State motor oil to Chex brand breakfast cereals.) Similarly, it's not hard to understand how monopolization can reduce the bargaining power of workers, who suddenly find themselves with fewer places to sell their labor.

America's problem in recent years hasn't been job destruction; it's been a fall-off in job creation.

The way corporate consolidation destroys jobs is clear enough, too—it dominates the headlines whenever a big merger is announced. Consider two recent deals in the drug industry. The first came in January 2009 when Pfizer, the world's largest drug company, announced plans for a $68 billion takeover of Wyeth. The second came in March 2009, when executives at number two Merck said they planned to spend $41.1 billion to buy Schering-Plough. Managers all but bragged of the number of workers who would be rendered "redundant" by the deal—the first killed off 19,000 jobs, the second 16,000.

Nevertheless, America's problem in recent years hasn't been job destruction, it's been a fall-off in job creation. Consolidation causes problems here, too, in a variety of ways. First, it can reduce the impetus of big firms to invest in innovation, a chief source of new jobs. The Austrian economist Joseph Schumpeter famously theorized that monopolists would invest their outsized profits into new R&D to enable themselves to innovate and thus stay ahead of potential rivals—an argument that defenders of consolidation have long relied on. But numerous empirical studies in recent years have found the opposite to be true: Competition is a greater spur to innovation than monopoly is. In one widely cited study, for instance, Philippe Aghion of Harvard University and Peter Howitt of Brown University looked at British manufacturing firms from 1968 to 1997, when the UK's economy was integrating with Europe and hence subject to the EU's antitrust policies. They found that on balance these firms became more innovative—as measured by patent applications and R&D spending—as they were forced to compete more directly with their continental rivals.

The opposite trend took place in some of America's biggest industrial firms in the years after 1981, when the Reagan administration all but abandoned antitrust enforcement. Many of the most successful U.S. companies adopted a winner-take-all approach to their industries that allowed them to short-change innovation and productive expansion. Prior to 1981, for instance, General Electric invested heavily in R&D in many fields, seeking to compete in as many markets as possible; after 1981 it pulled back its resources, focusing instead on gathering sufficient power to govern the pace of technological change.

Consolidation in the retail sector can also inhibit job growth. As behemoth retailers garner ever more power over the sale of some product or service, they also gain an ever greater ability to strip away the profits that once would have made their way into the hands of their suppliers. The money that the managers and workers at these smaller companies would have used to expand their business, or upgrade their machinery and skills, is instead transferred to the bottom lines of dominant retailers and traders and thence to shareholders. Or it may be simply destroyed through pricing wars. A good example is the pre-Christmas book battle between Amazon and Wal-Mart, in which the two giant conglomerates pushed down the prices of hardcover best sellers to lure buyers into their stores and Web sites. In many cases, the two companies actually sold the books for less than they bought them, treating them as "loss leaders" and expecting to recoup the loss through the sale of other, more expensive products. Although consumers welcomed the opportunity to pay $9.99 for the latest Stephen King novel priced elsewhere above $30, the move caused a near panic among publishers. Even though the low prices may have resulted in the sale of more books, the longer-term effect is to radically lower what consumers will expect to pay for books, which will in turn reduce the funds available to publishers to develop and edit future prospects.

Dominant firms can hurt job growth by using their power to hamper the ability of start-ups and smaller rivals to bring new products to market.

Another way that monopolization can inhibit the creation of new jobs is the practice of entrenched corporations using their power to buy up, and sometimes stash away, new technologies, rather than building them themselves. Prior to the 1980s, if a company wanted to enter a new area of business, it would typically have had to open a new division, hire talent, and invest in R&D in order to compete with existing companies in that area. Now it can simply buy them. There is a whole business model based on this idea, sometimes called "innovation through acquisition." The model is often associated with the Internet technology company Cisco, which, starting in the early '90s and continuing apace afterward, gobbled up more than 100 smaller companies. Other tech titans, including Oracle, have in recent years adopted much the same basic approach. Even Google, many people's notion of an enlightened, innovative corporate Goliath, has acquired many of its game-changing technologies—such as Google Earth, Google Analytics, and Google Docs—from smaller start-ups that Google bought out. As the falloff in IPOs [initial public offerings, when a company issues its stock to the public for the first time] over the last decade seems to confirm, one practical result of all this is that fewer and fewer entrepreneurs at start-up companies even attempt any longer to build their firms into ventures able to produce not merely new products but new jobs and new competition into established companies. Instead, increasingly their goal, once they have proven that a viable business can be built around a particular technology, is simply to sell out to one of the behemoths.

Finally, dominant firms can hurt job growth by using their power to hamper the ability of start-ups and smaller rivals to bring new products to market. Google has been accused of doing this by placing its own services—maps, price comparisons—at the top of its search results while pushing competitors in those services farther down, where they are less likely to be seen—or in some cases off Google entirely. Google, however, is a Boy Scout compared to the bullying behavior of Intel, which over the years has leveraged its 90 percent share of the computer microchip market to impede its only real rival, Advanced Micro Devices, a company renowned for its innovative products. Intel has abused its power so flagrantly, in fact, that it has attracted an antitrust suit from New York State and [has] been slapped with hefty fines or reprimands by antitrust regulators in South Korea, Japan, and the European Union [EU]. The EU alone is demanding a record $1.5 billion from the firm.

Good Job Opportunities Are Available in Some Fields Despite the Recession

Service Employees International Union

The Service Employees International Union (SEIU) is a fast-growing American union that represents workers in health care, public services, and property services.

For the millions of Americans who have lost their jobs or feared for their job security in the past couple of months, one might think there are simply no jobs to be had in this current economic down-spiral.

Although nobody's job is 100 percent secure, there *are* certain professions that have proven to be less sensitive to economic downturns. For the many Americans who spend their days scouring the classifieds or waiting in mile-long lines at career fairs, it's encouraging to know that there are job sectors that are still in need of educated employees right now. Here are a few bright spots:

Jobs Are Available in Certain Sectors

Health and education are at the top of the [Barack] Obama administration's—and our country's—list of priorities, so teachers and health care professionals are in high demand.

Of the 30 fastest growing professions reported by the Bureau of Labor Statistics [BLS], nearly half are related to the health care field, which saw a gain of 27,000 jobs in February [2009] alone. Highly in-demand occupations include nurses, medical assistants, physician assistants, home health aides, and medical records and health information technicians.

BLS has historically classified teachers as a recession-proof career field, and much like health care, there will always be a

Service Employees International Union, "America's Recession-Resistant Jobs," seiu.org, March 16, 2010. Reproduced by permission.

need for teachers. The National Center for Education Statistics predicts that in the next eight years, 2.8 million more teachers will be needed to join the 3.2 million existing teachers because of retirements, higher enrollment and teacher turnover.

More reasons to "Go Green": We all know it's time for America to invest in renewable energy for our country's future, and there is already a huge and growing sector working to fight global warming. The Obama administration is very focused on green job creation and clean energy initiatives that will work on harnessing all forms of solar, geothermal and wind power to double our renewable energy production by 2012 and advance sustainable growth.

It's reassuring to know that there are still job fields that stand a good chance of weathering this economic storm.

According to *Newsweek*, in one 2006 study released by the Renewable Energy Policy Project, researchers found that 2,000 businesses in Michigan could use wind turbine technology as an employment alternative for 34,000 ailing autoworkers by reorienting workers from their manufacturing jobs to jobs focused on creating renewable energy for the state. As the U.S. auto industry continues to decline, think about how many other states a project such as this could benefit. . . .

Jobs in "green" energy and the environmental sector will continue to see increased employment rates, to fill the green jobs that already exist as well as explore new technologies that will allow us to rely less on dwindling natural resources and preserve the environment.

Job Security in Security: The fact that we're in a recession doesn't lessen our country's need for security and law enforcement to ensure the safety and protection [of] its citizens. Jobs in America's Homeland Security and Defense Departments are increasing, with 80,000 more positions opening up over the next two years, as estimated by a report by the Partnership for

Public Service. Other sought-after positions include security guards, police officers, [and] international and transportation security experts.

Amongst the steady stream of discouraging economic news and dismal unemployment numbers, it's reassuring to know that there are still job fields that stand a good chance of weathering this economic storm.

America Will Face a Jobs Surplus in Ten Years

Barry Bluestone

Barry Bluestone is the dean of the School of Public Policy and Urban Affairs at Northeastern University and director of the university's Dukakis Center for Urban and Regional Policy. He also is a consultant to Civic Ventures, a national think tank with a focus on baby boomers.

World War II might have turned out differently if it weren't for Rosie the Riveter. When employers were desperate to fill factory jobs, millions of women joined the labor force and staffed America's "arsenals of democracy."

Today, with unemployment nearing 10 percent, it might seem far-fetched to suggest that we'll need Rosie's equivalent before the end of this decade. Yet, as the economy begins to recover, we will almost certainly see shortages in key occupations—and soon after, the demand for workers could outstrip supply in a broad range of industries, particularly within the so-called "social sectors."

Demographic Changes Ahead

To save the day, we'll need Rosies for a new era—older women and men willing to work longer in encore careers that shore up critical social and public services.

The reason for this remarkable turn of events is, simply, demographics:

- By 2018, the Census Bureau projects that there will be roughly 21.8 million more adults in the U.S. than in 2008.

Barry Bluestone, "A New Jobs Crisis on the Horizon," Salon.com, March 23, 2010. This article first appeared in Salon.com, at http://www.salon.com. An online version remains in the *Salon* archives. Reprinted with permission.

- The huge baby boom generation will continue to enter typical retirement age and live longer, while those reaching adulthood will come from the much smaller "baby bust" generation. That means that 95 percent of the net increase in population will be over 55, and more than half will be over 65.

- Only about 1 million adults age 18–54 will be added to the total of those normally expected to be in the workforce.

- Of the 21.8 million additional adults, just 9.1 million are likely to be in the workforce, assuming current labor force participation rates.

Meanwhile, once the jobs recession is over, the total number of additional jobs in the nation is expected to increase by over 15 million by 2018, which would leave a potential gap of 6 million unfilled jobs. Nearly half of these jobs will be in the social sectors: health care and social assistance, educational services, nonprofits, the performing arts, museums, libraries, and government.

If all 6 million potential jobs are left unfilled, the loss in potential output could total nearly $3 trillion over a five-year period.

A Need for Older Workers

This is where workers over 55 could become the Rosies of the 21st century.

For starters, boomers are not expected to retire at anywhere near the same rate as previous generations, and that could help fill the jobs gap. A 2008 MetLife Foundation/Civic Ventures survey found that half of Americans age 44 to 70 are interested in working longer in new jobs that contribute to improving the quality of life in their communities.

Two-thirds of those interested in "encore careers"—which combine personal meaning with continued income and social impact—say they are motivated by a desire to use their skills to help others. Their dream jobs: advocating for causes they believe in, working with kids, and preserving the environment.

These jobs are largely (though not exclusively) in the social sector of the economy. Providing opportunities for boomers to work in these jobs will increase the likelihood that they will work longer and help fill the impending jobs gap.

Filling the entire employment gap, however, will almost surely require that employers redesign and restructure jobs to appeal to an older workforce and consider new ways of retraining older workers for these positions.

It will also likely entail developing entirely new kinds of jobs—not yet accounted for in official labor statistics—that will both meet critical social needs and appeal to workers who want encore careers.

Experienced workers can be retrained to work in schools as adjunct teachers, mentors, tutors, and content advisers. They can work in the health field as community health workers, chronic illness coaches, medication coaches, and patient advocates. And they can work in the new green economy as energy auditors and conservation consultants.

Done right, there could be millions of encore career opportunities and a willing stable of older workers—Rosies for a new time—to fill them.

CHAPTER 2

Has the Government's Economic Stimulus Package Helped to Create Jobs?

Chapter Preface

Recession hit the American economy in 2007 and 2008 during the administration of President George W. Bush, and it continued into 2009, when Barack Obama assumed office. Laws were enacted and implemented by both administrations to stimulate the slowing economy and prevent a meltdown among banks and other institutions in the financial services sector. However, the most recent stimulus program supported by President Obama—the American Recovery and Reinvestment Act of 2009 (ARRA)—seems to be garnering the most attention and criticism today. One reason for this focus on ARRA may be that many of the stimulus-based loans have already been repaid—approximately $181 billion as of April 2010. In addition, experts as well as voters remain very worried about the economy because the nation's unemployment rate has stayed extremely high, close to 10 percent. People are closely watching, therefore, to see if President Obama's ARRA stimulus program fulfills its promise to save and create jobs and boost economic growth.

The government enacted the nation's first responses to the economic crisis during President Bush's administration—the Economic Stimulus Act of 2008 and the Emergency Economic Stabilization Act of 2008, which created the Troubled Assets Relief Program (TARP). President Bush's economic stimulus program, signed into law in February 2008, provided direct tax rebates to individuals and families in amounts up to $1,200 per couple plus $300 per dependent child, in order to boost consumer spending. The cost of this program was estimated at $152 billion. The TARP program, enacted in October 2008, provided up to $700 billion in federal funds to buy the assets of banks and other financial institutions in financial trouble due to the collapse of the housing market and housing securities.

When Barack Obama assumed the presidency in January 2009, the economy continued its downward slide, with some economists warning that it could develop into a second Great Depression, similar to the wrenching economic downturn the country suffered in the 1930s. President Obama, therefore, continued to administer the TARP program and also supported passage of a second economic stimulus bill to preserve and create jobs and promote economic recovery—the American Recovery and Reinvestment Act of 2009 (ARRA), enacted in February 2009.

Unlike President Bush's economic stimulus program, ARRA did not provide direct tax rebates to consumers. Instead, at an estimated cost of $787 billion, ARRA sought to ease the pain of the recession, create consumer spending, and promote long-term investments that would indirectly stimulate the economy by using two tools—expenditures and tax relief. For example, the bill included spending provisions to extend unemployment benefits for Americans who had lost jobs and to fund various projects. ARRA also included tax cuts, such as a provision extending a sales tax deduction to individuals who bought new cars. The scope of ARRA, however, is very broad, covering a wide range of initiatives intended to further technology, science, education, clean energy, and health, as well as make many repairs and upgrades to the country's infrastructure—that is, projects to repair and upgrade roads, bridges, railroads, public transit systems, Internet wireless and broadband, flood control, and power grids.

Economists' response to the $787 stimulus bill was mixed, with some economists supporting it, others calling for an even bigger government stimulus, and still others criticizing the massive deficit spending authorized by the legislation. As the recession continued, the debate shifted to whether the ARRA has been successful. One measure of success was suggested by officials in the Obama administration, who estimated that ARRA would create or save 3.5 million jobs over two years,

2009 and 2010—with more than 90 percent of those jobs in the private sector. Another benchmark of the bill's success, many economists agreed, was whether it would encourage consumer spending, which had slowed to a trickle as a result of high unemployment and falling real estate values. Some experts, however, thought that success would be measured by whether the economy as a whole continued to deteriorate or began to improve.

By the spring of 2010, a series of green shoots began to appear in the dismal U.S. economy, leading some policy makers and observers to declare that the recession was ending and that ARRA was working as intended. On February 17, 2010—the one-year anniversary of the ARRA—President Obama announced that the stimulus package had created or saved as many as 2 million jobs. In March 2010, U.S. manufacturing activity increased at the fastest rate in more than five years, and 190,000 jobs were added—the largest gain in three years. Also in early 2010, new claims for unemployment benefits declined over a span of five weeks, signaling that the pace of layoffs might be slowing. Other indicators suggested that industrial activity was improving and that consumers were beginning to spend again on big-ticket items like homes and motor vehicles. In an ABC News article by Matthew Jaffe, posted in April 2009, Ben Bernanke, chairman of the Federal Reserve, is reported to have declared that there were "tentative signs that the sharp decline in economic activity may be slowing." Supporters of the president were even more positive, arguing that the nation's economic decline probably reversed course sometime in 2009 and that the ARRA had helped keep the country from falling into a deep depression.

Critics, however, questioned these rosy pronouncements and noted that the nation's unemployment rate remained unacceptably high. The authors of the viewpoints in this chapter provide examples of the differing views of the ARRA and whether it has, or ever will, create jobs for American workers.

The Obama Administration Claims That Stimulus Legislation Has Created or Saved Almost 2 Million Jobs

Alec MacGillis

Alec MacGillis is a staff writer for the Washington Post, *an American daily newspaper published in Washington, D.C.*

The $787 billion economic stimulus package has created or saved between 1.7 million and 2 million jobs, but its impact on the economy ebbed slightly in the final quarter of 2009 compared with prior months, the White House said Tuesday night [January 12, 2010].

Effects of the Stimulus Package

Releasing the administration's second quarterly report to Congress on the stimulus's impact, Christina Romer, chairman of the Council of Economic Advisers, said a third of the tax cuts and spending in the package is out the door. Her office estimates that the stimulus added between 1.5 and 3 percentage points to the growth in gross domestic product [GDP, a measure of a country's total economic output] in the final quarter of 2009. That estimate, which is in line with other analyses, is lower than her office's estimate of stimulus-related impact in the third quarter, between 3 and 4 percentage points.

Administration officials said often last year that the stimulus's impact would be felt more over time as spending ramped up, but Romer said in a conference call with reporters that the drop-off in GDP impact was not unexpected. The biggest jolt to the GDP came with the first big surge of spending over the summer, she said, and job creation is now following.

Alec MacGillis, "Economic Stimulus Has Created or Saved Nearly 2 Million Jobs, White House Says," *The Washington Post*, January 13, 2010. Reprinted with permission.

"The most important bottom line is to say that close to 2 million jobs have been created or saved by the close of 2009, a truly stunning . . . effect of the act," she said. Still, she added, there is a need for additional spending to spur job creation, as President [Barack] Obama has called for.

Congressional Republicans have questioned the administration's claims about the stimulus's impact, pointing to the 10 percent unemployment rate nationwide. Romer's new figures are based on macroeconomic estimates, not reports filed by stimulus funding recipients, the next round of which is due later this month.

A New Way to Count Jobs

Separately, the White House has announced a change in the way those reports tally jobs, a response to critics that could make the reports more reliable but make it more difficult to gauge the stimulus's impact over time.

For months, economists and government watchdogs have warned that the job-creation reports should be taken with a heavy grain of salt. The administration deserves praise, they say, for trying to provide transparency in how the $787 billion package is being spent—whom the money is going to, and for what purpose—but trying to count the number of jobs created or saved may have been a fool's errand that needlessly undermined the credibility of the overall reporting effort.

This has proven especially true when it comes to "saved" jobs, which the administration says count as much as new jobs, since both keep people off the unemployment rolls. Recipients of stimulus money have used wildly different standards to estimate how many employees would have been laid off if not for the funding—some have reported every job in their business or agency as "saved," while others have reported zero jobs "saved," even after receiving very large contracts.

The job figures have other shortcomings. Since reporting is required only of the top two layers of funding recipients, the data do not capture jobs created further down the line of suppliers or subcontractors. And stimulus recipients have taken different approaches to counting jobs that are created or saved on a part-time or temporary basis.

New Reporting Rules

To address those concerns, the Office of Management and Budget recently issued new rules for reporting job numbers, aimed at ensuring more consistency. Most notably, the rules instruct recipients unsure how to count "saved" jobs to simply estimate how many employees in a given quarter were working on projects paid for by stimulus dollars, regardless of whether they would have been laid off otherwise.

But there is a downside: The shift in rules means that the numbers reported for the last quarter of 2009 and for the remainder of the stimulus cannot be compared with the job numbers from earlier in 2009. Going forward, recipients will no longer be expected to report a total count of jobs created or saved over time, but simply how many jobs were created or saved in a given quarter.

John Irons of the left-leaning Economic Policy Institute called the new rules a "huge improvement," saying that greater consistency among recipients is more important than having a cumulative jobs count. Even under the old rules, such a tally was going to be unreliable, he said, given the difficulty of counting jobs that only last a month or two.

"This is a better way to do it," he said. "You lose consistency between [the last two quarters] but you gain a whole lot of consistency across agencies. . . . It's a cleaner way to do things."

The American Recovery and Reinvestment Act Saved Americans from a Second Great Depression

Stephen Herzenberg

Stephen Herzenberg is an economist and the executive director of the Keystone Research Center, an economic research organization in Harrisburg, Pennsylvania.

Nearly a year ago, Congress took a decisive step to shore up an economy in free fall by passing the $787 billion stimulus bill. Since then, we have seen millions of Americans enter the ranks of the unemployed, billions of dollars spent on economic recovery, and quarterly growth swinging from the largest decline in a generation to positive territory in the same year.

Cut through all the numbers, though, and this is what you find: The American Recovery and Reinvestment Act saved us from plunging into a second Great Depression.

Impact of the Stimulus Bill

That's tough to fathom for many Pennsylvanians who are out of work or have lost their homes in the wake of the worst recession since the Depression. But on this first anniversary of the recovery act, let's take a look at a few of the legislation's achievements:

84,000 additional Pennsylvania jobs: Wall Street's excesses have robbed Pennsylvania of more than 200,000 jobs since the recession began two years ago. By contrast, the stimulus kept tens of thousands of Pennsylvanians—our neighbors, friends, and relatives—employed.

Stephen Herzenberg, "How the Stimulus Rescued America," Philly.com, February 17, 2010. Reproduced by permission of the author.

189,000 Pennsylvanians kept out of poverty: This is a major success by any measure. Extended unemployment benefits, tax credits for struggling families, and enhanced food stamp benefits, among other provisions, kept those Pennsylvanians hit hardest by the recession from falling into poverty last year.

$80 billion to U.S. consumers in the third quarter of 2009 alone: Is it any wonder that the economy started growing again when this money began making its way to Main Street?

I could give you more numbers, but you get the picture: The Recovery Act brought the economy back from the brink.

And these figures probably underestimate its impact, because they don't take market psychology into account. When the legislation passed, the economy was plunging at a pace similar to that of the 1930s. If Congress had sat on its hands, unemployment now could easily be 12 percent to 15 percent—and on its way to 20 percent.

More Action Needed

That being said, the work is not done. Thousands of Pennsylvanians are still unemployed, and we face a jobs crisis of mammoth proportions.

And yet that all-too-familiar pre-crisis paralysis has re-emerged in Washington. No longer faced with the potential collapse of the economy, politicians have lost the will to aid working families.

Our leaders need to muster the courage to act decisively again. Since private businesses and consumers aren't quite ready to drive our economic engine without a strong assist from government, we need a "Main Street Jobs Act" in Washington as well as in Harrisburg.

At the state level, Pennsylvania could tap into more than $600 million in additional federal funds for unemployment benefits, assistance for low-income families, and postsecondary-education grants for part-time workers. What are we waiting for?

With the enactment of the American Recovery and Reinvestment Act a year ago, Congress took the first major step toward bringing the economy back from the brink.

At both the state and national level, policy makers should mobilize more private investment in conservation and renewable energy. The green economy is the future, and Pennsylvania is ahead of many other states. Policies are already in place to mobilize $7 billion in private investment for green projects in Pennsylvania over the next three years, which is one reason our economy is doing better than other states'. Now we need to build on that progress.

We also need state and federal policies that lift the incomes of middle-class families—such as a higher minimum wage and requirements that publicly funded green jobs pay decently. Remember: Flagging family incomes, combined with consumption financed by unsustainable borrowing—including loans against inflated home values—helped get us in this mess. Restoring middle-class income growth will pull us out— and keep us out by sustaining private consumption and investment for the long term.

With the enactment of the American Recovery and Reinvestment Act a year ago, Congress took the first major step toward bringing the economy back from the brink. And it worked.

Now we need our leaders to take additional steps to assure that the economy delivers for regular Pennsylvanians and Americans. Otherwise, unemployment will remain high for years to come.

The Number of Jobs Created by the Stimulus Bill Is Overstated

L.D. Jackson

L.D. Jackson is a blogger and the creator of Political Realities, a political blog site.

Remember how Barack Obama and his hordes of aides descended on Washington, D.C., before he even took the oath of office and began making the push and the sell for a massive economic stimulus package? To the tune of $787 billion, they told the American people that it was necessary and vital to any economic recovery. They told us how it would preserve jobs and even how it would create new ones.

That has been about ten months ago and there has been more than one report on the effectiveness of the stimulus package. One of the latest reports credits the recovery package with creating or saving 14,506 jobs with the spending from just one federal office, Health and Human Services. Sounds great, right? Well, as it turns out, not so much.

Inaccurate Reports of Jobs Saved

The Associated Press [AP] has been looking at the accuracy of some of these reports and it has found that the above number has been overstated by as much as two-thirds. The reason for this overstatement is the way these reports are playing fast and loose with the definition of some of the terms used in the reports. For instance, in the case mentioned above, federal officials instructed local officials to count pay raises as jobs saved. That's right, they gave people raises and counted it as a job being saved.

L.D. Jackson, "How Well Has the Economic Stimulus Worked?" Political Realities, November 5, 2009. Reproduced by permission.

"That's more than ridiculous," said Antonia Ferrier, a spokeswoman for Republican House Minority Leader John Boehner.

Most of the inflated figures were like those cited in the 935 saved jobs reported by the Southwest Georgia Community Action [Council] in Moultrie, Ga. The agency, like hundreds of others collecting Head Start money, claimed all its existing employees' jobs were saved because they received a pay raise with the stimulus cash.

[President Barack Obama's] promise of an open and transparent government continues to be ignored.

Similar claims led to overstating by more than 9,300 the number of jobs saved with more than $323 million in stimulus money distributed by the Health and Human Services' Administration for Children and Families, the AP's review found.

More than 250 other community agencies in the U.S. similarly reported saving jobs when using the money to give pay raises, pay for training and continuing education, extend employee work hours or buy equipment, according to their spending reports.

The Georgia program inflated the numbers even further by claiming the recovery money saved more jobs than the number of people it actually employs. The agency employs 508 people but claimed 935 jobs were saved because of confusion over government reports.

For once, I would like a little honesty from Washington, but here is what Health and Human Services spokesman Luis Rosero had to say about the accounting practices.

If I give you a raise, it is going to save a portion of your job.

That is about as lame of an excuse for inaccurate reporting as I have ever heard. I don't have a problem per se with giving people pay raises, although I do wonder why they didn't try to create more jobs. I do believe the American taxpayers at least get an honest and accurate report of how our money is being spent.

There have been problems with the previous reports on the effect of the economic stimulus package, but President Obama assured us they would be corrected. That doesn't appear to be the case with the latest report and I have to wonder this out loud. How long does he expect the American people to continue taking his word? I am afraid his promise of an open and transparent government continues to be ignored.

Government Spending Does Not Create Jobs

Brian Riedl

Brian Riedl is the lead budget analyst for the Heritage Foundation, a conservative think tank.

Proponents of President Barack Obama's $787 billion stimulus bill continue to insist that the massive government bailout played a decisive role in moving the economy out of the recession. Yet assuming no destructive government actions, the economy's self-correction mechanism was widely expected to move the economy out of recession in 2009 anyway. With a parade of "stimulus" bills the past two years (going back to President George W. Bush's tax rebate in early 2008), it was entirely predictable that some would link the expected end of the recession to whichever stimulus bill happened to come last.

Stimulus Facts

Indeed, President Obama's stimulus bill failed by its own standards. In a January 2009 report, White House economists predicted that the stimulus bill would create (not merely save) 3.3 million net jobs by 2010. Since then, 3.5 million more net jobs have been lost, pushing the unemployment rate above 10 percent. The fact that government failed to spend its way to prosperity is not an isolated incident:

- During the 1930s, New Deal lawmakers doubled federal spending—yet unemployment remained above 20 percent until World War II.

- Japan responded to a 1990 recession by passing 10 stimulus spending bills over 8 years (building the

Brian Riedl, "Why Government Spending Does Not Stimulate Economic Growth: Answering the Critics," The Heritage Foundation, Backgrounder no. 2354, January 5, 2010. Reproduced by permission.

largest national debt in the industrialized world)—yet its economy remained stagnant.

- In 2001, President Bush responded to a recession by "injecting" tax rebates into the economy. The economy did not respond until two years later, when tax rate reductions were implemented.

- In 2008, President Bush tried to head off the current recession with another round of tax rebates. The recession continued to worsen.

- Now, the most recent $787 billion stimulus bill was intended to keep the unemployment rate from exceeding 8 percent. In November, it topped 10 percent.

Undeterred by these repeated stimulus failures, President Obama is calling for yet another stimulus bill. There is every reason to expect another round to fail as miserably as the past ones, and it would bury the nation deeper in debt.

The Stimulus Myth

The economic theory behind the stimulus builds on the work of John Maynard Keynes eight decades ago. It begins with the idea that an economic shock has left demand persistently and significantly below potential supply. As people stop spending money, businesses pull back production, and the ensuing vicious circle of falling demand and production shrinks the economy.

Keynesians believe that government spending can make up this shortfall in private demand. Their models assume that—in an underperforming economy—government spending adds money to the economy, taxes remove money from the economy, and so the increase in the budget deficit represents net new dollars injected. Therefore, it scarcely matters how the dollars are spent. Keynes is said to have famously asserted that a government program that pays people to dig and refill ditches would provide new income for those workers to spend and circulate through the economy, creating even more jobs and income.

The Keynesian argument also assumes that consumption spending adds to immediate economic growth while savings do not. By this reasoning, unemployment benefits, food stamps, and low-income tax rebates are among the most effective stimulus policies because of their likelihood to be consumed rather than saved.

Taking this analysis to its logical extreme, Mark Zandi of Economy.com has boiled down the government's influence on America's broad and diverse $14 trillion economy into a simple menu of stimulus policy options, whereby Congress can decide how much economic growth it wants and then pull the appropriate levers. Zandi asserts that for each dollar of new government spending: temporary food stamps adds $1.73 to the economy, extended unemployment benefits adds $1.63, increased infrastructure spending adds $1.59, and aid to state and local governments adds $1.38. Jointly, these figures imply that, in a recession, a typical dollar in new deficit spending expands the economy by roughly $1.50. Over the past 40 years, this idea of government spending as stimulus has fallen out of favor among many economists. As this [viewpoint] shows, it is contradicted both by empirical data and economic logic.

Economic data contradict Keynesian stimulus theory.

The Evidence Against the Stimulus

Economic data contradict Keynesian stimulus theory. If deficits represented "new dollars" in the economy, the record $1.2 trillion in FY [fiscal year] 2009 deficit spending that began in October 2008—well before the stimulus added $200 billion more—would have already overheated the economy. Yet despite the historic 7 percent increase in GDP [gross domestic product, a measure of a country's total economic output] deficit spending over the previous year, the economy shrank by 2.3 percent in FY 2009. To argue that deficits represent new money injected into the economy is to argue that the economy would have contracted by 9.3 percent without this "infusion" of added deficit spending (or even more, given the Keynesian multiplier effect that was supposed to further boost the impact). That is simply not plausible, and few if any economists have claimed otherwise.

And if the original $1.2 trillion in deficit spending failed to slow the economy's slide, there was no reason to believe that adding $200 billion more in 2009 deficit spending from the stimulus bill would suddenly do the trick. Proponents of yet another stimulus should answer the following questions: (1) If nearly $1.4 trillion budget deficits are not enough stimulus, how much is enough? (2) If Keynesian stimulus repeatedly fails, why still rely on the theory?

This is no longer a theoretical exercise. The idea that increased deficit spending can cure recessions has been tested repeatedly, and it has failed repeatedly. The economic models that assert that every $1 of deficit spending grows the economy by $1.50 cannot explain why $1.4 trillion in deficit spending did not create a $2.1 trillion explosion of new economic activity.

Why Government Spending Does Not End Recessions

Moving forward, the important question is *why* government spending fails to end recessions. Spending-stimulus advocates claim that Congress can "inject" new money into the economy, increasing demand and therefore production. This raises the obvious question: From where does the government acquire the money it pumps into the economy? Congress does not have a vault of money waiting to be distributed. Every dollar

Congress injects *into* the economy must first be taxed or borrowed *out* of the economy. No new spending power is created. It is merely redistributed from one group of people to another.

Congress cannot create new purchasing power out of thin air. If it funds new spending with taxes, it is simply redistributing existing purchasing power (while decreasing incentives to produce income and output). If Congress instead borrows the money from domestic investors, those investors will have that much less to invest or to spend in the private economy. If they borrow the money from foreigners, the balance of payments will adjust by equally raising net imports, leaving total demand and output unchanged. Every dollar Congress spends must first come from somewhere else.

Taking dollars from one part of the economy and distributing [them] to another part of the economy will not expand the economy.

For example, many lawmakers claim that every $1 billion in highway stimulus can create 47,576 new construction jobs. But Congress must first borrow that $1 billion from the private economy, which will then *lose at least as many jobs*. Highway spending simply transfers jobs and income from one part of the economy to another. As Heritage Foundation economist Ronald Utt has explained, "The only way that $1 billion of new highway spending can create 47,576 new jobs is if the $1 billion appears out of nowhere as if it were manna from heaven." This statement has been confirmed by the Department of Transportation and the General Accounting Office (since renamed the Government Accountability Office), yet lawmakers continue to base policy on this economic fallacy.

Removing water from one end of a swimming pool and pouring it in the other end will not raise the overall water level. Similarly, taking dollars from one part of the economy and distributing [them] to another part of the economy will not expand the economy.

University of Chicago economist John Cochrane adds that:

First, if money is not going to be printed, it has to come from somewhere. If the government borrows a dollar from you, that is a dollar that you do not spend, or that you do not lend to a company to spend on new investment. Every dollar of increased government spending must correspond to one less dollar of private spending. Jobs created by stimulus spending are offset by jobs lost from the decline in private spending. We can build roads instead of factories, but fiscal stimulus can't help us to build more of both. This form of "crowding out" is just accounting, and doesn't rest on any perceptions or behavioral assumptions.

Second, investment is "spending" every bit as much as is consumption. Keynesian fiscal stimulus advocates want money spent on consumption, not saved. They evaluate past stimulus programs by whether people who got stimulus money spent it on consumption goods rather than save it. But the economy overall does not care if you buy a car, or if you lend money to a company that buys a forklift.

Government spending can affect long-term economic growth, both up and down. Economic growth is based on the growth of labor productivity and labor supply, which can be affected by how governments directly and indirectly influence the use of an economy's resources. However, increasing the economy's productivity rate—which often requires the application of new technology and resources—can take many years or even decades to materialize. It is not short-term stimulus.

In fact, large stimulus bills often reduce long-term productivity by transferring resources from the more productive private sector to the less productive government. The government rarely receives good value for the dollars it spends. However, stimulus bills provide politicians with the political justification to grant tax dollars to favored constituencies. By increasing the budget deficit, large stimulus bills eventually contribute to higher interest rates while dropping even more debt on future generations. . . .

What Government Policies Do Affect Growth?

While government spending merely displaces private spending dollar for dollar in the short run, it can have a long-term impact on productivity. Similarly, tax policy can also affect productivity and growth.

Government Spending Can Have a Long-Term Impact. Although it cannot immediately increase economic growth, government spending can have a long-term impact. Economic growth results from producing more goods and services (not from redistributing existing income), and that requires productivity growth and growth in the labor supply. Productivity growth requires some combination of: (1) a more educated and efficient workforce; (2) more private physical capital, such as factories and tools; (3) increased use of new technology; (4) more public infrastructure like roads and other utilities; and (5) markets to set prices and rule of law to enforce contracts. Government's effect on economic growth is determined by its effect on productivity and labor supply.

Only in the rare instances where the private sector fails to provide those inputs in adequate amounts is government spending necessary. Government spending on education, physical infrastructure, and research and development, for instance, could increase long-term productivity rates—but only if government invests more competently than businesses, nonprofit organizations, and private citizens would have if those investment dollars had stayed in the private sector. Historically, governments have rarely outperformed the private sector in generating productivity growth. Thus, mountains of academic studies show that government spending typically *reduces* long-term economic growth.

Even most programs that could increase productivity would take too long to be considered stimulus. Education spending will not affect productivity until the student has graduated and entered the workforce (and it is not clear that additional spending improves productivity anyway). New roads, highways, and bridges can take more than a decade to complete before they can transport people and goods. These policies should not be considered short-term stimulus spending.

Tax Policy's Strong Effect on Economic Growth. Taxes can affect growth, although not for the reason many people believe. Many tax cutters commit the same fallacy as do government spenders when asserting that tax cuts spur economic growth by "putting spending money in people's pockets." Similar to government spending, the tax-cut cash does not fall from the sky. It comes from reduced investment and a higher trade deficit (if financed by budget deficits) or from government spending (if offset by spending cuts).

However, certain tax cuts can add substantially to productivity. As stated above, economic growth requires that businesses produce increasing amounts of goods and services, and that requires consistent business investment and a growing, productive workforce. Yet high marginal tax rates—defined as the tax on the next dollar earned—create a disincentive to engage in those activities. Reducing marginal tax rates on businesses and workers will increase incentives to work, save, and invest. These incentives encourage more business investment, a more productive workforce by raising the after-tax returns to education, and more work effort, all of which add to the economy's long-term capacity for growth.

Thus, not all tax cuts are created equal. The economic impact of a tax cut depends on how much it alters behavior to encourage labor supply or productivity. This productivity standard is the same as the one applied to government spending in the previous section.

Tax rebates fail to increase economic growth because they are not associated with productivity or work effort. No new income is created because no one is required to work, save, or invest more in order to receive a rebate. In that sense, rebates that write each American a check are economically indistinguishable from government spending programs. In fact, the federal government treats rebate checks as a "social benefit payment to persons." They represent another feeble attempt at creating new purchasing power out of thin air rather than focusing on productivity.

Focusing on productivity growth builds a stronger economy over the long term—and leaves America better prepared to handle future economic downturns.

Tax rebates in 1975, 2001, and 2008 all failed to create economic growth. By contrast, large reductions in marginal tax rates in the 1920s, 1960s, and 1980s were each followed by large surges in economic growth. More recently, the 2003 tax-rate reductions immediately reversed the job losses, sinking stock market, declining business investment, and sluggish economic growth rates that had followed the 2000 recession. These gains continued until unrelated economic developments brought the most recent recession in December 2007.

The Need to Focus on Productivity Growth

All recessions eventually end. The U.S. economy has proved resilient enough to eventually overcome even the most misguided economic policies of the past. Yet it would be fallacious to credit the stimulus bill for any economic recovery that inevitably occurs in the future. According to Keynesian theory, a $1.4 trillion budget deficit should have immediately overheated the economy. According to the White House, the stimulus should have created 3.3 million net jobs. Instead, the economy remained in recession and 3.5 million more net jobs were lost. By every reasonable standard, the stimulus failed.

H.L. Mencken [an American journalist] once wrote that "complex problems have simple, easy to understand, wrong answers." He may as well have been referring to the idea that Congress can foster economic growth simply by "injecting" money into the economy. Government stimulus spending is not a magic wand that creates jobs and income. Repeated failed attempts in America and abroad have shown that governments cannot spend their way out of recessions. Focusing on productivity growth builds a stronger economy over the long term—and leaves America better prepared to handle future economic downturns.

The American Recovery and Reinvestment Act Is Not Reaching Workers of Color

Jason Reece, Matt Martin, Christy Rogers, and Stephen Menendian

Jason Reece is a senior researcher for the Kirwan Institute, an interdisciplinary research institute located at Ohio State University in Columbus, Ohio. Christy Rogers is a senior research associate; Matt Martin is a GIS/Planning specialist; and Stephen Menendian is a senior legal associate at the Kirwan Institute.

Facing an escalating economic crisis, newly inaugurated President [Barack] Obama signed the historic American Recovery and Reinvestment Act [ARRA] (commonly referred to as "the stimulus") on February 17, 2009. The $787 billion stimulus bill was designed to create and preserve jobs, spur economic growth, and be administered with a particular focus on transparency and accountability. The stimulus bill made explicit reference to "assist those most impacted" by the recession. Has ARRA provided relief to our hardest-hit communities? Has ARRA worked to promote greater racial and socioeconomic equity in our nation? One year into the implementation of ARRA we find mixed results, and offer critical lessons learned from the ARRA experience. In addition, we provide specific recommendations for achieving the goals of the Recovery Act, generating jobs and broadening prosperity, and reducing our racial and economic divide.

An Uneven Economic Crisis

The brunt of unemployment, layoffs, social service and education budget cuts, foreclosures, and bankruptcies has been borne by groups already marginalized by the mainstream

Jason Reece, Matt Martin, Christy Rogers, and Stephen Menendian, "ARRA & the Economic Crisis—One Year Later: Has Stimulus Helped Communities in Crisis?" Kirwan Institute, February 2010. Reproduced by permission.

economy. In particular, the racial impacts of the recession and housing crisis have been extreme. One in five children were living in poverty in 2008, and poverty rates for children of color are climbing above 40% in some states. While one in ten workers are unemployed nationally, one in six black workers and one in eight Latino workers are unemployed. Nearly half of all subprime loans went to African American and Latino borrowers, even though many qualified for prime loans. African American and Latino homeowners are expected to lose $164–$213 billion in assets due to the housing crisis. While much of our analysis focuses on race, it is important to note that other factors, such as geography and gender, impacted the way in which the recession burdened already vulnerable communities. The impact of the recession on children has already been severe and will potentially be long-lasting. The percentage of children in poverty is likely to peak at 21% in 2010. Neighborhoods and communities are also being reshaped by the detrimental impacts of the housing crisis and recession.

ARRA One Year Later: Protecting Vulnerable Populations from Devastating State Budget Cuts

A significant portion of ARRA was dedicated to offsetting state budget shortfalls, many of which could have resulted in drastic cuts to critical services for marginalized populations. In this regard, ARRA prevented massive budget cuts to critical services that would have further harmed vulnerable populations. Analysis of the impact of ARRA suggests that several ARRA programs will help alleviate the growing poverty across the nation by expanding existing tax credits and financial assistance programs. However, more fiscal peril and potential budget cuts could be on the horizon. While the Recovery Act will provide more than $100 billion to offset state budget deficits in 2010 and 2011, even with this funding states are expecting another $267 billion in additional budget deficits for

2010 and 2011. As a result, the draconian budget cuts predicted for 2009 may loom again in 2010.

Despite job production claims and growth in the US domestic product, national unemployment has increased during 2009.

ARRA One Year Later: Failing to Address Joblessness for Marginalized Racial Populations

Job production was a primary goal of ARRA, and the ability of ARRA to offset rising unemployment is a critical measuring stick to assess ARRA's impact. Despite job production claims and growth in the US domestic product, national unemployment has increased during 2009. Between February 2009 and December 2009, the national unemployment rate increased from 8.2% to 10% and the number of unemployed increased from 12.7 million to 15.2 million people. As recently reported by the Associated Press, there were 6.1 unemployed workers for every available job in December of 2009, a figure which is nearly double the rate of 3.1 unemployed workers for every available job opening at the end of 2008. Workers of all races experienced increasing unemployment during 2009, with the number of unemployed black and Latino workers increasing by nearly 1.5 million. Latinos experienced the fastest rate of unemployment growth during 2009, with unemployed Latino workers increasing by 38%.

Recently released January 2010 unemployment figures indicate some changing trends, with a decline in national unemployment figures, but continuing growth in unemployment for some populations. While the national unemployment rate declined from 10% to 9.7% (indicating a decrease of 430,000 unemployed workers), unemployment increased for some racial groups. White unemployment has started to decrease (from a peak of 9.4% in October 2009 to 8.7% in January 2010), while black unemployment rates continue to rise (from 15.5% to 16.5% during the same time period). Latino unemployment rates have also decreased slightly but remain very high, decreasing from 13.1% in October 2009 to 12.6% in January 2010. The new divergence in unemployment rates is particularly troublesome, suggesting our economy's modest economic gains from late 2009 are not reaching our most economically vulnerable populations. While overall unemployment has started to decline (and decline for white workers), black workers may soon reach the 2010 unemployment rate which was once projected to occur if a stimulus or recovery bill was not enacted. This suggests that many of the employment gains from ARRA are not reaching workers of color.

ARRA One Year Later: Underperforming in Producing Minority Procurement & Contracting

Contracting and procurement are the primary ways ARRA can directly benefit private businesses and employers. Minority and disadvantaged business contracting is a critical source of job and wealth creation for marginalized groups and communities. Many concerns have been raised about the ability of minority firms to successfully compete for contracts. Although consistent state-level data on ARRA contracting to minority firms is not widely available, figures from federal procurement indicate troubling and disparate contracting patterns. While black-, Latino-, and women-owned businesses represent 5.2%, 6.8%, and 28.2% of all businesses respectively, as of February 1, 2010, they had only received 1.1%, 1.6%, and 2.4% of all federally contracted ARRA funds. Of the $45 billion in direct federal contracts allocated by February 1, 2010, less than $2.4 billion (5% of the total) were allocated to black-, Latino-, and women-owned businesses.

The Housing Crisis One Year Later: Inadequate Federal Response

The subprime lending and foreclosure fiasco, a key driver of the current economic recession, continues to destabilize families and neighborhoods across the country. The Neighborhood Stabilization Program (NSP), which allocates funds to communities to buy and rehabilitate vacant homes, has been criticized as too little, too late. In many communities, the number of vacant homes is several *thousand* times that of the number of homes potentially salvaged by NSP. Second, because the program directs the funds to be used in hardest-hit neighborhoods (a principle that seems sound on its face), it may be putting its drops in the wrong bucket: Rather than trying to salvage a few homes in an overwhelmed neighborhood, it may be better to move foreclosed families into rehabilitated homes in more stable neighborhoods.

In fact, the federal government has addressed the foreclosure crisis primarily outside of the stimulus bill, through the Department of Treasury programs. By all accounts, even the Treasury's programs have not performed well enough. With millions of families facing foreclosure, comparatively few have received permanent loan modifications under Making Home Affordable, which includes both "HARP" [Home Affordable Refinance Program] and "HAMP" [Home Affordable Modification Program]. HARP was designed for borrowers who are "underwater," or owe more than their home is worth. Unfortunately, many homeowners are so far underwater they cannot qualify for a refinance; nor do they have the ability to pay closing costs, given that they have exhausted themselves financially trying to keep current on the mortgage. As of October 2009, about 130,000 of the 5 million potentially eligible loans were modified under HARP. With regard to HAMP, out of the 3 to 4 million households targeted by the program, 110,000 have been approved for permanent modifications as of late December, with a great many more in temporary modifications (the administration reported in January that a total of 850,000 homeowners have received temporary or permanent HAMP modifications). Two macro-scale forces are weakening the programs, including continually falling home prices and increasing joblessness. The voluntary nature of the programs, and the fact that mortgage companies can collect lucrative fees from long-term delinquency, has slowed servicer and lender action.

In short, the scale and scope of the crisis has overwhelmed the federal response. The administration should now consider more significant actions, such as requiring equity write-downs and giving bankruptcy judges the right to amend mortgages. In broader terms, the subprime crisis and resultant economic tsunami requires nothing short of a systemic reconfiguration of federal priorities, including effective bank regulation and consumer protections.

Moving Forward

Despite ARRA's inability to fully counter the economic crisis facing marginalized communities, the need for continued federal action, investment and leadership is critical. As documented in this [viewpoint], indicators for socioeconomic health in many communities are indicating widespread hardship for many marginalized communities, especially communities of color. At the state level, ARRA funds (and future policy efforts to reverse the economic crisis facing marginalized communities) must be refocused in several ways.

- *Improve Tracking of ARRA Resources and Outcomes.* Rather than scaling back job-tracking efforts, there should be additional measures which consider the quality and duration of employment, as well as the race, gender, and zip code of job recipients.

- *Increase Small and Minority Business Participation.* Unbundle large contracts for small businesses. Breaking up large projects will allow for more small business participation in the recovery. Set and mandate specific MBE [minority business enterprise] and DBE [disadvantaged business enterprise] goals for every department.

- *Ensure That Hard-Hit Communities Experience Job Impact.* Use targeted reinvestment in hard-hit areas, first source hiring, apprenticeship and job training. Increase employment opportunities for ex-offenders.

In addition, federal reforms are needed to assure that federal agency plans are consistent with all of the goals of ARRA, including its emphasis on those most impacted by the economic crisis. A review of the agency plans raises two broad, systemic concerns that require immediate attention. First, it appears that agency programs funded by ARRA may insufficiently reflect ARRA's priorities. There is a greater need to more carefully align agency programmatic activities with ARRA's goals, particularly its emphasis on job creation and assistance to those most affected by the crisis. Secondly, the mandate to expend ARRA funds as quickly as possible, with special priority given to "shovel-ready" projects and projects receiving private investment, may be giving short shrift to civil rights compliance, particularly Title VI and Title VIII of the Civil Rights Act of 1964.

Finally, an equitable jobs bill is still required to stem the economic crisis facing marginalized communities. A future jobs bill would ideally support community development in urban and minority-majority areas, which have been damaged most severely by the recession and credit crises. The bill should explicitly protect and provide for those who are especially vulnerable to joblessness and lack of access to job markets. Any new federal job creation strategy that invests in our nation's infrastructure should invest in other critical community infrastructure (outside of road investments) as well, such as transit, schools and parks. It should develop new recruitment and training standards that help new workers get into jobs, and help minority- and women-owned businesses get a fair opportunity to win contracts. Finally, measures must be taken to ensure that marginalized communities are brought fully into the green economy, as "green job" initiatives begin to take shape in both federal and state policy.

CHAPTER 3

Will Green Jobs Solve
America's Job Shortage?

Assessing the Economic Impact of Green Jobs Is Difficult

Marc Gunther

Marc Gunther is a veteran journalist, speaker, writer, and consultant with a focus on business and sustainability who contributes to various publications, including Fortune *magazine and the Web site Greenbiz.com.*

As the battle over climate change legislation heats up, several Big Green groups—the Environmental Defense Fund [EDF], the Natural Resources Defense Council [NRDC] and the Sierra Club—are rolling out TV and Internet ads designed to persuade voters that regulating greenhouse gas emissions will create green jobs. David Yarnold, the president of EDF's Action Fund, sums up the message in an e-mail: "Carbon Caps = Hard Hats." Clever....

These ads take what may be an even more devilishly complicated issue, climate change regulation, and use images of brawny construction workers to turn it into an even shorter sound bite: "Green jobs."...

Maybe I missed it, but did you hear an environmental message in either of those ads?

The Green Jobs Debate

Of course, there's research to support the claims about green jobs. In the interests of full disclosure, I need to say here that I've been doing some freelance work for EDF and NRDC— organizations I admire a great deal. But these claims about green jobs deserve greater scrutiny.

Last June [2008], for example, the BlueGreen Alliance, Sierra Club, NRDC and the steelworkers issued a green jobs report from the Political Economy Research Institute (PERI) at the University of Massachusetts, Amherst. It said:

> ... millions of U.S. workers—across a wide range of familiar occupations, states, and income and skill levels—will benefit from the project of defeating global warming and transforming the United States into a green economy.

A second report from PERI, issued last September under the auspices of the Center for American Progress, got more granular. In my home state of Maryland, for example, the authors project that a $100 billion green economic recovery program would create 36,739 jobs. They would be created in such industries as building retrofitting, mass transit and freight rail, smart grid, wind power, solar power and advanced biofuels.

There's an emerging economic consensus that the costs of dealing with climate change are significant but manageable—and that given the risks, those costs are likely worth paying.

It sounds great, doesn't it?

Not according to the four lawyers and economists who produced "7 Myths About Green Jobs," a 97-page report published by the University of Illinois College of Law. They argue that "the green jobs literature is rife with internal contradictions, vague terminology, dubious science, and ignorance of basic economic principles." Studies by conservative think tanks go further, claiming that climate legislation will destroy millions of jobs. A 2008 Heritage Foundation study claimed that passage of last year's Lieberman-Warner bill would create "extraordinary perils for the American economy" and cause annual job losses of between 500,000 and 1,000,000 after a few years of job gains. (This report was thoroughly discredited by NRDC.) The best thing I've read about this debate (and one of the most balanced) is ... a fine *Slate* article by Eric Pooley, my former editor at *Fortune*, who finds that there's an emerging economic consensus that the costs of dealing with climate change are significant but manageable—and that given the risks, those costs are likely worth paying.

Something for Nothing

My point here is not that economists disagree. My point is that the climate change debate shouldn't be about green jobs. It's intellectually dishonest to pretend that we can forecast, with any degree of accuracy, the impact of a complicated government policy on a dynamic global economy decades into the future. Both sides know that their projections are based on a host of assumptions, which may or may not come true. What if we decide as a nation to turn to nuclear energy as a source of low-carbon power? That probably won't create many long-term jobs. What if there's a breakthrough in the solar PV [photovoltaic] business in China? That may not bring green jobs here. Are farmers who grow corn for ethanol doing green jobs? That hasn't turned out so well.

Let's get real: We can't predict oil prices 12 months out. Last spring, virtually no one anticipated the global financial crisis of last fall. And we are projecting the number of green jobs that will be created or lost on a state-by-state basis by a law that won't take effect until 2012? Who are we kidding?

I called Russ Roberts, an economist at George Mason University who hosts the fine *EconTalk* podcast, for some guidance on how to think about green jobs and the economics of climate regulation. "Creating green jobs is easy," he told me. "We could employ millions of people picking up litter, and we could make them very good-paying jobs if we want. But of course that would make us poorer as a nation. There's a cost to providing those jobs that would have to be borne by other people in the economy."

It's not just the cost of higher taxes that needs to be factored into the equation, he noted. To the degree that the government makes policy that favors, say, vast construction of wind turbines throughout the upper Midwest, the people doing those jobs will be drawn from somewhere else, maybe even from more productive work. If policy leads to the hiring of thousands of contractors to do energy efficiency, the cost of building a new home or renovating your basement may go up because many of the good construction workers are busy.

"As voters and citizens and readers, what we want to think about is the big picture—are we moving in the right direction when it comes to environmental policy?" Roberts says. Put another way, are we spending enough money today to head off the threat of global warming in the future? Because if anyone tells you that we can deal with climate change at no cost, they probably shouldn't be trusted.

Maybe that's what bothers me about the green jobs ads. They're like political campaign ads. They promise something for nothing. They treat the voters like children. They're emotional and not educational. And they're not helping to build a movement around climate change.

Other than that, they're fine.

And I do hope they work.

A Green Economy Can Create Millions of Good Jobs

Apollo Alliance

The Apollo Alliance is a coalition of labor, business, environmental, and community leaders working to catalyze a clean energy revolution that will put millions of Americans to work in a new generation of high-quality, green-collar jobs.

The movement to make American cities more sustainable, efficient and livable is perhaps the greatest new engine for urban economic growth, innovation and job creation in many decades.

The American Solar Energy Society estimates that in 2006 alone, renewable energy and energy efficiency were responsible for $970 billion in industry revenues and 8.5 million jobs. This number will grow exponentially if our nation commits itself in earnest to reducing carbon emissions and making economy-wide improvements in energy efficiency.

A Green Labor Shortage

Unfortunately, America's growing green economy faces a looming labor shortage in sectors like manufacturing, construction and installation. In a 2005 survey by the National Association of Manufacturers, 90 percent of respondents indicated a moderate to severe shortage of qualified, skilled production employees like machinists and technicians. Similarly, the National Renewable Energy Laboratory has identified a shortage of skills and training as a leading barrier to renewable energy and energy efficiency growth. This labor shortage is only likely to get more severe as baby boomers skilled in

Apollo Alliance, *Green for All, Center for American Progress, and Center on Wisconsin Strategy*, "Green-Collar Jobs in America's Cities: Building Pathways Out of Poverty and Careers in the Clean Energy Economy," apolloalliance.org, March 13, 2008. Reproduced by permission.

current energy technologies retire; in the power sector, for example, nearly one-quarter of the current workforce will be eligible for retirement in the next five to seven years.

Clearly if America is to rise to the global energy challenge, and capture the economic opportunity it represents, we need to prepare the next generation of Americans for the important work that lies ahead. Green jobs exist, and are growing, in a range of industries and at every skill and wage level. Many are in the skilled trades: manufacturing, construction, operation and maintenance, and installation. Most are "middle-skill" jobs, requiring more education than a high school diploma, but less than a four-year degree. Some are a bridge to high-skill professional jobs or entrepreneurial opportunities; others are perfect entry-level or transitional jobs for urban residents looking for a pathway out of poverty. In short, green jobs are the kind of family-supporting jobs that once anchored the American middle class, but in the industries of the future: industries like wind turbine manufacturing, solar panel installation, energy efficiency retrofits, and green building. . . .

Developing Green Economies

This [viewpoint] focuses on local green jobs in clean energy industries—energy efficiency, renewable energy, alternative transportation, and low-carbon fuels. Specifically, it offers guidance on how cities can link residents to *green-collar jobs*: family-supporting, career-track jobs in green industries. We hope it will help cities across America develop strategies to expand their green economies and connect the promise of the global clean energy future to the practical realities of local green economic and workforce development.

If your city or region wants to find ways to leverage local environmental, economic development, and workforce development programs to grow the green-collar jobs of the future, this [viewpoint] is for you. It explains the link between embracing visionary public policies and investments, and expanding demand for local green-collar workers. It outlines the importance of building on existing workforce and economic development initiatives to meet this demand. It lays out ways to link traditional training partnerships to Green Jobs Corps or similar initiatives that offer pathways out of poverty. And it shows how the success of your green-collar jobs effort can help build a broader-based constituency for even more ambitious clean energy initiatives in the years to come.

The field of green economic and workforce development is a new and exciting one. The strategies outlined in this [viewpoint] build on the hard work being done right now in cities across America.... Thank you for your interest in, and commitment to, building a clean energy future for America.

Green Jobs Will Offer Hope to Many Unemployed Americans

Bracken Hendricks, Andrew Light, and Benjamin Goldstein

Bracken Hendricks and Andrew Light are senior fellows at the Center for American Progress (CAP), a progressive think tank. Benjamin Goldstein is a policy analyst at CAP.

Our country faces two immense, interrelated challenges: Charting a course to economic recovery and tackling the threat of global warming. Both are moral imperatives that require immediate action in order to fulfill our future obligations to our children. Meeting these challenges head on now and into the future is straightforward—begin a robust and aggressive transition towards a clean energy economy. This transition will leverage new investment streams to build low-carbon infrastructure, catalyze private sector innovation, and lay the foundation for sustainable, long-term economic growth. Building the clean energy economy will also create millions of new green jobs, offering hope to many Americans who are out of work or facing possible layoffs. With major energy and climate policy decisions on the horizon, and the excitement over green jobs growing, we offer answers below to four common questions.

1. What is a green job?

The short answer: Green jobs enhance environmental quality, build a vibrant clean energy economy, and help to expand the American middle class.

The long answer: Green jobs are today's jobs but repurposed and expanded to build a sustainable low-carbon economy. Most green jobs will be in occupations that people already work in today. Constructing wind farms creates jobs

Bracken Hendricks, Andrew Light, and Benjamin Goldstein, "A Green Jobs Primer: Job Creation in a Clean Energy Economy," Center for American Progress, April 4, 2009. This material was created by the Center for American Progress. www.americanprogress.org.

for sheet metal workers and industrial truck drivers. Energy efficiency retrofits for buildings employ roofers and insulators. And expanding mass transit systems employs electricians and dispatchers. Green jobs are not an entirely new job sector. Akin to more familiar blue-collar jobs, this new class of employment refers to certain types of productive activities rather than a specific job classification.

Green jobs encompass a wide breadth of skill sets and pay scales. The bulk is good-paying, middle-skill jobs accessible to all Americans.

What's more, green jobs are inherently local and difficult to outsource. Green jobs involve transforming today's homes, offices and factories and investing in new, low-carbon infrastructure. This work is impossible to push offshore because it must be performed on-site. Making buildings more energy efficient, constructing mass transit lines, installing solar panels and wind turbines, expanding public green space, and growing and refining advanced biofuels all must take place right here in America.

2. Are green jobs only low-paying jobs?

The short answer: No. Green jobs encompass a wide breadth of skill sets and pay scales. The bulk is good-paying, middle-skill jobs accessible to all Americans.

The long answer: Our research demonstrates that green jobs are broadly distributed across the entire spectrum of the economy. In a side-by-side comparison of job creation from green investments versus investments in the oil industry, we demonstrated that nearly four times more jobs are created overall at every step in the pay scale and across every skill level. Green jobs represent a wide range of points of entry into meaningful, long-term employment, and can provide ladders into the middle class for lower-skilled workers if career advancement and workforce training opportunities are integrated into our larger economic development strategies.

In fact, green jobs are blue collar and white collar alike. Green jobs are not only production line, construction, and manufacturing jobs. Green businesses will need secretaries, managers, and accountants, too. High-technology endeavors will offer new opportunities in green design, engineering, and finance. Such a diverse spectrum of job creation is precisely what we need in an economy suffering from its worst downturn since the Great Depression.

3. Do gains in green jobs cause losses in other sectors of the economy?

The short answer: No. A clean energy economy will result in net job creation because green investments are domestic, have a large multiplier effect, and create work that is skill and labor intensive.

The long answer: Investments in renewable energy and energy efficiency can create twice as many jobs per unit of energy and per dollar than traditional fossil fuel investments by redirecting money previously spent on wasted energy, pollution, and imported fuel toward advanced manufacturing, modern infrastructure, and skilled labor. In the beginning stages, green jobs will simply result in the creation of new jobs that did not exist before, putting people to work without displacing existing sectors. In the medium term, some particularly polluting sectors of the economy experience employment downturns, which is why we must devise smart policies to transition affected workers.

But one day all good jobs will be green jobs as we build an economy where productivity and competitiveness are contingent on increased environmental stewardship and efficient use of all resources, including energy. Moreover, initial public investments in green infrastructure will "crowd-in" private capital. This follows a time-tested script that helped build the railroads, the national highway system, and enabled the development of the Internet revolution. In each case, strategic public investment enabled market transformation and the growth of new industries and vast new opportunities for economic growth and wealth generation.

4. Are green jobs the result of picking technological "winners"?

The short answer: No. A clean energy economy will reward efficiency, low-carbon energy, and environmental stewardship. Any and all technologies can compete and contribute in this transformed market.

The long answer: Building a clean energy economy means fixing broken markets where the costs of pollution are passed onto future generations. Setting strong market signals with smart policies through a combination of investment and regulation will allow the market to decide the most appropriate technologies without distorting real consumer choices.

These policies will also spur a huge wave of innovation as the private sector steps up to meet the challenges of solving global warming and reducing our dependence on polluting fossil fuels. That's the ultimate promise of new green jobs in a clean energy economy.

Clean Energy Jobs Will Provide a New Source of Economic Growth

Heather Taylor

Heather Taylor served as the deputy legislative director for the Washington, D.C., office of the Natural Resources Defense Council (NRDC), an environmental organization. She now lives in San Francisco, where she continues to work with NRDC and the NRDC Action Fund.

Last week [February 1, 2010], two conservative Republican senators, James Inhofe of Oklahoma and John Barrasso of Wyoming, called for an independent probe of the IPCC [Intergovernmental Panel on Climate Change]—the international scientific body that summarizes the latest climate science—and asked the Senate to halt all climate action until that happens.

The senators claim that because there were some errors included in the IPCC's 2007 report—for instance, how quickly the Himalayan glaciers might melt—the entire phenomenon of climate change must now be questioned.

Climate Action Makes Good Political Sense

I am not a scientist by training, but even I know their reasoning doesn't hold up. The few errors that have been uncovered in the thousand pages or so of the IPCC report have nothing to do with the science of whether and why climate change is occurring. Instead, those errors are about a few specific projections about what might happen in the future.

Saying we should discard the entire thrust of climate scientists because of a couple of sloppy projections is like saying

Heather Taylor, "Why Climate Change Deniers Should Still Support Green Energy," NRDC Action Fund, February 10, 2010. Reproduced with permission from the Natural Resources Defense Council. This article has been edited from the original.

the concept of evaporation is in doubt because a handful of scientists mistakenly said Lake Mead evaporates faster than we thought.

Senators Inhofe and Barrasso are trying to use this excuse to ignore the IPCC. But it won't be so easy to get around the National Oceanic and Atmospheric Administration, the National Academy of Sciences, the National Science Foundation, the Pentagon, the National Intelligence Council, the World Health Organization, and the CIA [Central Intelligence Agency].

Each and every one of these world-class institutions has concluded that climate change is a serious threat.

But let's face it, people like Inhofe will never be persuaded by scientific argument. Climate denial is an article of faith for them, and I don't believe in arguing about people's religion.

We need individuals and companies to invest in something on a massive scale in order to instill confidence and create jobs. Clean energy and climate solutions fit the bill.

But I do argue politics, and on the issues that matter most to Americans right now—jobs, the economy, and security—climate action makes good political sense.

So even if Inhofe's posturing about the IPCC gives some senators pause, they can't ignore the following facts.

Climate Action Will Result in Positive Things

Fact: Climate Action Will Create Jobs: Every senator running for reelection this year has one question to answer: Where are the jobs? Voters are hungry for opportunities, and a clean energy and climate bill will deliver them.

Clean energy jobs are growing 2.5 times as fast as traditional jobs right now. Indeed, according to economists at the

University of California, the climate bill that passed the House of Representatives last June [2009] could generate nearly 2 million new jobs.

Why so many opportunities? Clean energy industries require more people than those in the fossil fuel industry. In fact, for every $1 million spent on clean energy, we can create 3 to 4 times as many jobs as if we spent the same amount on fossil fuels.

Some senators have the defeatist attitude that China will capture the clean energy market because of its low wages. In fact, a recent study by the EPIA [European Photovoltaic Industry Association] found that 75 percent of all solar energy jobs are in installation and maintenance and the trend is similar for other clean energy technologies. You can't outsource the job of building a wind farm or making an office more energy efficient.

But here is another fact: the only way to get these jobs benefits is to pass a clean energy and climate bill. Without that bill, businesses don't get the incentive to invest in job-heavy, low-carbon energy sources. And without those jobs, senators will have a much harder time talking to their voters.

Fact: Climate Action Will Generate Economic Growth: Many economists believe that we need a new engine for growth. We need individuals and companies to invest in something on a massive scale in order to instill confidence and create jobs.

Clean energy and climate solutions fit the bill. Annual investments in the global clean energy market could reach $106 to $230 billion a year in 2020 and as much as $424 billion in 2030 (from NRDC [Natural Resources Defense Council] President Frances Beinecke's book, *Clean Energy Common Sense: An American Call to Action on Global Climate Change*). What other sector is offering that kind of growth right now?

But in order to unleash private investment, companies need the right incentives. Peter Darbee, the head of PG&E [Pacific Gas and Electric, an energy company], wrote in the

Capitol Hill newspaper *Politico* that America's utilities need about $2 trillion over the next 20 years to modernize electrical infrastructure. But, he said, companies are delaying capital spending because, while they know climate legislation is coming, they don't know when and they don't know what it will look like. In the meantime, they are holding onto their cash and postponing job creation.

Darbee urged Congress to pass a climate bill because, he wrote, it will "clear the way for many companies to accelerate near-term investment and job creation. Longer term, it would enhance America's economic competitiveness and national security."

Fact: Climate Action Will Strengthen Our National Security: The Christmas bomber put security back on the list of top priorities for many American voters. It was a terrible reminder that distant unrest can wash up on our shores.

And that's what the Department of Defense is worried about when it comes to climate change. A few weeks ago, the Pentagon released its Quadrennial Defense Review—its official assessment of military risks—and it called climate change a threat to national security that "may spark or exacerbate future conflicts," and labeled global warming "an accelerant of instability." The Central Intelligence Agency and the National Intelligence Council came to similar conclusions.

If we stay on our current path—ignoring climate change and continuing to fuel it with our oil addiction—the risks will only grow. Americans spent a record $450 billion on imported oil in 2008—$1,400 for every man, woman, and child in this country. This money was sent overseas to places like Saudi Arabia, Venezuela, and Nigeria. Do you think those regimes have our best interests in mind?

Retired Navy Vice Admiral Dennis McGinn explained it like this: "Our growing reliance on fossil fuels jeopardizes our military and effects a huge price tag in dollars and potentially lives. . . . In our judgment, a business-as-usual approach constitutes a threat to our national security."

A clean energy and climate bill will disarm that threat, protect our servicemen and women, and keep billions of dollars here in America.

Senators Inhofe and Barrasso can argue over the science as much as they want. The scientific community can and will defend the science behind climate change. While they have that debate, there are lots of additional, incredibly important reasons to get started. . . . So, let's not wait.

President Obama's Green Jobs Plan Will Do More Harm than Good

Nick Loris

Nick Loris is a research assistant at the Heritage Foundation's Roe Institute for Economic Policy Studies, a conservative think tank.

On the campaign trail Barack Obama promised if he were elected president, he would create 5 million "green-collar" jobs. Today [January 8, 2010] President Obama announced $2.3 billion in tax credits for a clean energy economy will ostensibly create 17,000 jobs. "Building a robust clean energy sector is how we will create the jobs of the future," he said in a speech this afternoon.

The Problems with Green Jobs

Make no mistake; this government-run plan will kill more jobs than it aims to create.

There are a number of serious problems with the goal to create green jobs, and Europe's unfavorable results with renewable energy should raise red flags in the United States. And cap and trade, which is sold by President Obama, [Speaker of the U.S. House of Representatives] Nancy Pelosi, among others as the ultimate jobs bill, is in reality the ultimate jobs destroyer.

Less Bang for Your Buck: Sure, the government can create jobs. They can use our taxpayer dollars to hire workers to dig holes and fill them back up. But if there's no net gain in productivity and wealth, the job is a waste. For instance, we could replace all of the world's mechanized agriculture equipment with hoe-wielding farmers, and that would create jobs. But it would also significantly reduce productivity and efficiency. The economic reasoning for switching from more efficient machinery to less efficient human capital is such a baseless plan any politician suggesting it would be laughed out of office.

Thus far, the effort to create or save jobs with a green initiative hasn't been very successful.

Yet that is the exact premise of the green jobs boondoggle. The government wants to mandate and subsidize labor intensive, inefficient, and expensive power sources. But the problem is that if it takes more labor and capital to produce renewable energy, there is a net cost to the economy. Proponents of wind and solar [power] argue this is a good thing. Apparently they forgot the there's-no-free-lunch-lesson you learn in Economics 101. Government spending will create some jobs to build windmills and solar panels and work at biomass plants but this diverts labor, capital and materials from the private sector that could be used more efficiently to create even more jobs. In effect, government-subsidized green jobs destroy jobs elsewhere.

Cap and trade, while not part of the green stimulus, is being marketed as such. Because of higher energy prices, some jobs will be destroyed completely while others will move overseas where carbon capping isn't in their country's agenda and therefore the cost of production is cheaper. The Heritage Foundation's Center for Data Analysis found that, for the average year over the 2012–2035 time line, job losses will be 1.1 million greater than without a cap-and-trade bill. By 2035, there is a projected 2.5 million fewer jobs.

Green Stimulus Already Failing: Thus far, the effort to create or save jobs with a green initiative hasn't been very successful. In Baltimore [Maryland], for instance, stimulus dollars have been spent to patch roads, install newer furnaces and paint rooftops white to conserve energy. According to the *Washington Post's* Alec MacGillis, none of these projects, as well as others, have created a single job. Another example is in the state of Indiana, where companies have "weatherized 82 homes out of its three-year goal of 25,000, and reported zero new jobs from the spending."

Learning from Europe's Mistakes: A research institute located in Germany recently released a study on the economic impacts of that country's green energy initiative. Commissioned by the Institute for Energy Research (IER), the report finds [that] . . . per worker subsidies for solar industry jobs are as high as $240,000.

Spain is a country President Obama says the U.S. should replicate when it comes to energy policy, saying, "they're making real investments in renewable energy." But real investments aren't necessarily good investments. Another IER-commissioned study coming out of King Juan Carlos University in Madrid by Gabriel Calzada found that, for every green job created, 2.2 jobs in other sectors have been destroyed. Furthermore, Spain's government spent $758,471 to create each green job and used $36 billion in taxpayer money to invest in wind, solar, and mini-hydro from 2000–2008. The country's unemployment rate is currently at 19.4%.

Allowing Green Energy to Compete Freely

The economically rational way to create jobs and expand green energy is to allow them to compete freely in the market, end dependence on the government, and eliminate regulatory barriers to entry. Like all energy sources, green energy should be able to live or die on its own two feet.

In time and with the proper policies in place, renewable energy might be inexpensive and efficient. If the private sector can create wealth by hiring green laborers for renewable energy projects (absent federal handouts), it will do so. The U.S.

Chamber of Commerce's "Project No Project" lists all the renewable energy plans not moving forward and the groups that are opposing them. The NIMBY [Not in My Backyard], regulatory litigation problems make it difficult, not just for renewable sources but [for] all sources of energy, [and] stifle real job creation and economic growth. To fix this Congress and the administration should:

1. *Peel back regulations.* Reduce the unnecessary regulatory red tape that holds up renewable energy ventures and makes them prohibitively more expensive and deters investment. Establishing regulatory certainty would allow businesses to plan financing for the future rather than to be hit unexpectedly with unforeseen costs.

2. *End energy subsidies.* Subsidies create complacency within the industry and direct money that could be used more efficiently elsewhere. The private sector investment in energy research is actually larger than many might think. True breakthroughs in energy technology take time but the private sector has been generating marginal improvements in efficiency for decades.

3. *Limit litigation.* Creating a manageable time frame for groups or individuals contesting energy plans would avert potentially cost-effective ventures from being tied up for years in lawsuits.

We've heard the green jobs rhetoric before and we'll likely hear it again, but that doesn't make it a good idea. It's a profoundly wasteful use of taxpayers' money and will do much more to hurt the economic recovery than to help it.

Green Jobs Are Dependent on Government Spending and Artificial Markets

Max Schulz

Max Schulz is a senior fellow at the Manhattan Institute, a New York City think tank.

In early October [2009] the federal government released its monthly employment statistics. The numbers were stunningly dismal. According to the Labor Department, the economy lost 263,000 jobs in September, and unemployment ratcheted up to nearly 10 percent. The jobs report included an additional bit of bad news: a revision of the numbers from March 2008 to March 2009 revealed the economy had lost 800,000 more jobs than previously thought.

So where are all the green jobs we have been promised? It wasn't enough that the [Barack] Obama administration claimed that passing the massive stimulus bill in February was necessary to prevent unemployment from reaching as high as 9 percent (if only!). But the White House and its supporters also assured us of an employment boom coming from a government-sponsored transition to a post–fossil fuel economy. Well, the government sponsorship is in evidence, thanks in large part to the stimulus bill authorizing more than $60 billion for energy and environmental projects. A green-shooted economic recovery, however, so far is not.

Problem with the Green Economy

One of the problems with the green economy is that there is no accepted definition of what constitutes a green job. A report issued by Vice President [Joe] Biden says green jobs are

Max Schulz, "About Those Green Jobs . . ." *The American Spectator*, October 29, 2009. Reproduced by permission.

"employment that is associated with some aspect of environmental improvement." But because this definition is so broad, the report states, "it is impossible to generate a reliable count of how many green jobs there are in America today."

Is your job green? The guy weatherizing your house has a green job, as does the scientist in the lab cooking up the next alternative to oil. But so might the truck driver in the fuel-guzzling 18-wheeler who is carting mammoth wind turbine parts along hundreds of miles of Texas highway. As well as, arguably, the United Nations official who jets all over the globe to hector about climate change.

The obvious dilemma with . . . estimates [of green job creation] is that they depend on government action to spring these jobs into being.

Not having any baseline to start from doesn't stop advocates from predicting the number of jobs that their enlightened policies will create. The president himself has promised to create 5 million green jobs by spending $150 billion over ten years. The [progressive think tank] Center for American Progress suggested that federal outlays of $100 billion over a two-year period would create a million green jobs. The Apollo Alliance [an alliance of businesses and groups in favor of a greener economy] said $500 billion would be necessary to create 5 million green jobs. (Asked by the *Wall Street Journal* to explain the vast discrepancy between President Obama's expensive jobs figure with the Apollo Alliance's three-times-more expensive figure, an official with the organization replied, "Honestly, it's just to inspire people.")

The obvious dilemma with these estimates is that they depend on government action to spring these jobs into being. This makes clear that the economy otherwise does not value them enough to create them as part of a robust economic climate. Green jobs don't really exist in the free economy. The green economy is, in essence, an artificial construct, legislated into existence by politicians unbothered by the costs involved. The jobs boom of the [President Ronald] Reagan years was never predicated on how much money the federal government would shell out. The coming green boom is. And it isn't just the money that federal and state authorities will shower on everything from weather-stripping to smart meters to biofuels production. Government also wants to guarantee the markets for uneconomical green-energy sources, as with so-called renewable portfolio standards that mandate the amount of costly green power that utilities must provide.

Yet another absurd example of the government "creating" green jobs was New York City's breathless announcement last week that it would double citywide green employment—from 6,500 to 13,000 jobs—by establishing itself as the center of the global carbon permit trading market. These are jobs that will exist only by virtue of Congress passing an onerous and economically debilitating cap-and-trade bill. In much the same way that every new set of regulations brings more work for lawyers and accountants, cap and trade will require clerks and financial experts and other functionaries to ensure the smooth operation of a scheme that the market neither wants nor values. Forget all the harping on Wall Street and the financial community over the past year's financial crisis; the "greed-is-good" brigade will be doing the Lord's work when it starts trading credits in an artificial market created by politicians.

A Green Jobs Boomlet

Still, those jobs are in the future. Most green jobs seem to be. Though the stimulus bill was passed in February, and billions of dollars started being dispersed months ago, green jobs proponents don't point to any progress on their part in combating the economic downturn. The jobs they promise are always yet to be created.

At the [National] Clean Energy Summit in Las Vegas a few months back, Senate Majority Leader Harry Reid announced, "Today, August 10th, here in Las Vegas, we're firing the first shots of a new revolution to regain that prosperity and restore that leadership—a clean energy revolution that will create millions of jobs across America." The first shots? Then what was the $60 billion gift to the renewable energy industry in the stimulus bill?

[Green jobs will] cost us a bundle, and will be worth a whole lot less to society than what the government paid for them.

It turns out that the green jobs promise can mean all things to all people. And all pressure groups. The Women's Economic Security Campaign, for instance, is turning its focus to green jobs as a pathway out of poverty for low-income women. Inner-city poverty groups likewise think the green jobs express can revitalize the ghetto, and can also help return ex-cons to the mainstream. For groups like these, green is the new uplift.

For others, green jobs is a vehicle for interest groups to get theirs. Labor wants the newly created green jobs to go to union members to help pad dwindling rolls. The American Public Transportation Association claims that spending on their projects is a surefire way to create green jobs. Well, of course they do.

Meanwhile, none of the news coming out of Washington about jobs in the real economy is encouraging. The American Recovery and Reinvestment Act [ARRA] appears to have been far less stimulative than advertised. In time, one imagines, employment figures in the green economy will head north. How can they not, given the fact the government is guaranteeing them? So, we will have our green job boomlet. But there's a hitch, which is that those green jobs come with a hefty price tag. They'll cost us a bundle, and will be worth a whole lot less to society than what the government paid for them.

Green Jobs Will Ruin the American Economy

Rich Trzupek

Rich Trzupek is a chemist, consultant, and writer who writes extensively about environmental and science topics and is a contributor to FrontPage Magazine *and several other online and print publications.*

As a certain frog once observed, it ain't easy being green. It's not profitable either, but as environmentalists and their supporters in government retool their message they dearly want us to believe that a "green economy" will fill everyone's pockets with greenbacks. Recent experience, not to mention common sense, shows that this is nonsense. Nonetheless, the [Barack] Obama administration, environmental groups and many mainstream media outlets are pushing "green jobs" and a "green economy" as ways to simultaneously solve America's economic woes while avoiding any possible harm to the environment.

Rebranding Green Jobs

At a Chicago City Club luncheon a few weeks ago, an official with the Chicago Department of the Environment was introduced to the crowd. She waved happily and dutifully parroted the environmental movement's latest slogan:

"What's good for the environment is good for the economy!"

And we have this: Al Gore wants to "repower America!" Warming to the theme, the president of the United States would have America believe that green jobs and green power will not only put money in your pocket, they are the wave of the future. China's doing it, the president says, do we want to be left behind?

Rick Trzupek, "Green Jobs: The Road to Ruin," *FrontPage Magazine*, March 25, 2010. Reproduced by permission.

Except that China's not doing it. They're paying lip service to "green power" as they happily build big coal-fired power plants at the rate of one per week, because it's pretty obvious to the Chinese that cheap power is better for their economy than politically correct power.

The push to "go green" has been responsible for much of Spain's recent economic woes.

The purported nirvana of a green economy is the predictable response to "Climategate," "Glaciergate," "Amazongate" and all the rest of the revelations that have caused the public to doubt that our planet actually needs saving. If the science isn't really settled and has in fact been manipulated for the sake of an agenda (Climategate), is there really an environmental crisis to worry about? If glaciers aren't going to melt in the next twenty-five years (Glaciergate), can the Intergovernmental Panel on Climate Change be trusted? If the rain forests are doing just fine, thank you (Amazongate), is the situation as bad as global warming alarmists have led us to believe? It's 2010 and panic just isn't selling as well as it did five years ago. Accordingly, the global warming crowd is rebranding their product, saying in essence that even if you don't believe in "climate change" it still makes sense to go green, because doing so will make everyone more wealthy along the way.

The Cost of Green Jobs

Arguably, no Western nation has done more to go green than Spain. Indeed, President Obama has pointed toward Spain as the model of the sort of economy that the United States should aspire to create, one that relies heavily on renewable fuels for power. But, how has that worked out for Spain? In the midst of a worldwide recession, the Spanish economy stands out, because it is in worse shape than most, with unemployment hovering at around twenty percent. According to a study conducted by Dr. Gabriel Calzada, an economics professor at [King] Juan Carlos University in Madrid, the push to "go green" has been responsible for much of Spain's recent economic woes. Calzada concluded that every green job created in Spain cost 2.2 traditional jobs. A green economy, it would seem, is hardly a formula for prosperity.

But one shouldn't need the Spanish experience to realize that a green economy is inevitably a red ink economy. Common sense is all that is necessary. Wind power, the most popular form of renewable power, is fifty percent to one hundred percent more expensive than coal-fired power. Why? Because the people who develop wind farms have to pay off the bank notes for building all of those expensive windmills, shell out cash for operating and maintenance costs and fund the not inconsiderable costs of the infrastructure required to hook the windmills up to the grid. Add in the fact that you still have to back up wind farms with conventional forms of energy, like gas turbines, and wind power is inevitably more expensive than burning coal or natural gas. But for government subsidies and incentive programs, no one would be stupid enough to build a single windmill.

If implemented . . . green schemes won't create wealth; they will instead sap America's riches, and we will all be the poorer for it.

The same may be said of solar power, which is, by nature, horrendously expensive and inefficient, as well as biofuels, which often consume more energy than they produce, and a host of other green, renewable schemes to repower America in shades of green. There's a reason that we need legislation to create a green economy: There is no free market, economic incentive to otherwise do so.

It's worth noting that I myself have held what may be termed a "green job" for over twenty-five years. Without environmental legislation, I would have had to pursue a career doing something that was actually productive. As it happened, I have spent my professional life poring over EPA [Environmental Protection Agency] regulations, pushing through the piles of paperwork that the regulatory system demands on behalf of my clients and carefully studying the latest environmental research. The only reason that a job like mine exists is that America has built a regulatory structure to protect the environment that is so enormously complex and impossible to understand that specialists are needed to figure out what the heck the average business person has to do in order to avoid the wrath of the EPA.

The worst part of this state of affairs is that, by and large, it's not the big, bad corporations that require the services of people like me. Big power companies, oil refiners, etc. can afford their own specialists who can lead those large corporations through the regulatory maze. Instead, it's the small companies—those who can least afford it—that are forced to look for outside help. They can't afford their own dedicated environmental professionals, thus they are forced to fork over cash that they could have otherwise been using to improve their businesses and create jobs in order to retain expert consultants that can keep aggressive regulators at bay.

Leftists like Obama find nothing troubling in the green jobs paradigm, whether it means building expensive windmills or forcing small businesses to pay for specialists who keep the creeping hand of the bureaucracy at arm's length. To liberals, the economy is a zero-sum game, so what could be wrong about redistributing billions of dollars? For those of us who believe that wealth is created, rather than something that exists in the abstract sense, the idea of a green economy is something far more sinister. If implemented, these green schemes won't create wealth; they will instead sap America's riches, and we will all be the poorer for it.

CHAPTER 4

What Should the United States Do to Create Greater Job Growth?

Chapter Preface

As 2010 began, America's economy was stuck in a recession, with few signs of recovery and persistently high unemployment. In response to the nation's job crisis, President Barack Obama called jobs his number one focus in his State of the Union address and proposed a number of job-creation ideas to build upon the $787 billion economic stimulus bill passed in February 2009. One idea was a plan to encourage businesses to hire new workers by easing credit and providing a series of tax cuts. In addition, the president proposed using funds from the Troubled Asset Relief Program (TARP), an earlier bank bailout program, to lend more money to small businesses. Another option was an energy rebate program, called Home Star, which offered financial incentives for home weatherization with the goal of stimulating hiring in the construction and manufacturing sectors. President Obama also called for an extension of unemployment benefits, emergency aid for states and cities, help for seniors, and health care aid for unemployed workers.

Some of the president's proposals have yet to be enacted into law, including the Home Star energy rebate program, but others were acted on by Congress. For example, legislation was passed to continue the extended unemployment benefits program—a federal program that provides thirteen to twenty weeks of additional benefits on top of regular unemployment benefits provided according to each state's unemployment rate. The bill, passed in April, authorized this extended unemployment program until June 2, 2010.

On March 17, 2010, Congress passed a $17.6 billion jobs bill, called the Hiring Incentives to Restore Employment (HIRE) Act, designed to encourage businesses to hire and retain new workers. The bill gave employers an exception from the 6.2 percent Social Security payroll contribution for each worker hired through the end of 2010, as long as the employee has been out of work for at least sixty days. In addition, the legislation allowed businesses to take an additional $1,000 income tax credit for every new employee kept on the payroll for fifty-two weeks and made it easier for businesses to take tax deductions for purchases of equipment. Other provisions in the March 2010 jobs bill authorized $20 billion in federal funds for highway and mass transit programs and encouraged expanded investments in schools and clean energy. The goal was to help small business owners and, at the same time, create new jobs both in small businesses and construction industries. The president was able to get bipartisan support for the legislation, but to do so, the bill was scaled back from an earlier $150 billion version.

Critics, mostly Republicans, complained that the HIRE Act would create precious few jobs and have little impact on overall unemployment. At most, some commentators pointed out, the bill would produce perhaps 250,000 new jobs by the end of 2010—a tiny number considering that 8.4 million U.S. jobs had been lost since the beginning of the recession. Democrats, however, praised the bill and characterized it as just one step in a series of efforts to encourage private sector job growth. Other steps that might be considered by Congress, for example, include additional business tax breaks for research and development and programs to provide small businesses with increased access to credit. Various other job proposals have also been introduced in Congress, including the Local Jobs for America Act, a $75 billion bill that would help cities by funding local government and nonprofit employees who provide important services such as education, public safety, child care, and health care.

The authors of the viewpoints in this chapter present a variety of views about actions that should be taken to boost job growth in America.

Innovation, Research, and Education Are the Keys to Job Creation

Anthony Mason

Anthony Mason is a business correspondent for CBS News.

Look for the road signs leading to a job recovery in America, and as CBS News business correspondent Anthony Mason reports, you'll find the country at a crossroads.

The U.S. has to find new ways to rebuild its workforce.

Where America Stands

For 23 straight months now, the U.S. economy has been hemorrhaging jobs. The report card isn't pretty.

One in six Americans, 17 percent, is underemployed. That's nearly 25 million people who are out of work, have given up looking, or been forced to take a part-time job.

The recession has wiped out 15 percent of our manufacturing workforce. That's more than 2 million jobs that will likely never come back.

The damage to America's labor force is both deep and profound. The Great Recession has obliterated a decade's worth of job growth. Economic prosperity is impossible without job growth. But in the decade just ended, we created less than half a million new jobs. In each of the previous four decades, the economy generated at least 18 million jobs.

"It's going to take a really long time for recovery," said Heidi Shierholz, a labor economist at the Economic Policy Institute [an economic research organization]. "We are going to have elevated unemployment for probably the next five years."

Anthony Mason, "The Future of Jobs in America: Innovation, R&D, and Education are Keys to Job Creation," CBSNews.com, January 3, 2009. Reproduced by permission.

Estella and Mike Pesapane are jet engine technicians. But Pratt & Whitney [a manufacturer of aircraft engines] plans to shut down their plant this year, and ship most of those 1,000 jobs overseas.

"All my experience, what do I do with it?" asks Mike Pesapane. "I gotta start all over. I gotta go back to school."

What's happened? The United States is still the world's strongest economy, but our competitive edge is eroding.

Innovation

Analysts say innovation must be the first in a three-pronged strategy to replace lost American jobs.

In the 1960s, launching the Apollo space program created millions of jobs and led to innovations like fuel cells and freeze-dried food.

That same decade, the Defense Department began building a computer network that became the Internet.

Justin Rattner is chief technology officer for Intel [a computer technology company]. He's the man who developed the first supercomputer to process one trillion operations per second.

"Tens of millions of jobs were created from the innovations around the Internet. It's time to do that again," Rattner said. "Now is the time to be investing, not saving. You don't save your way out of a recession. You invest your way out of it."

Research and Development

That's the second part of the solution for job creation: research and development. But government spending on research and development actually fell by 3.8 percent in 2009.

That's the worst drop in 30 years. Just when growing young industries like Printed Electronics are looking for money.

Education has to be the final part of the strategy for job growth.

Andy Hannah's Pittsburgh company, Plextronics, which makes low cost solar panels, has quickly expanded to 70 employees. But the Europeans have pumped $1 billion into research, while the U.S. has done virtually nothing.

"We are behind," Hannah said. "This can bring a real manufacturing base back to the United States."

Intel just committed $7 billion to build new factories in Arizona, Oregon and New Mexico, to make the next generation of semiconductor devices. That will mean thousands of new jobs, but Justin Rattner said they may be hard to fill.

"Are you telling me that even if we innovate and create new products, we don't necessarily have the people to do the jobs?" Mason asked.

"That's right," Rattner replied. "We're not graduating nearly the numbers of engineers that are coming out of universities in China and India and elsewhere."

Education

That's why education has to be the final part of the strategy for job growth. In a recent study, 15-year-olds in the U.S. ranked 21st out of 30 countries in science scores.

What are they up against? India's high tech giant, Infosys, just opened a $120 million training center: the biggest corporate college in the world.

Infosys CEO [chief executive officer] Kris Gopalakrishnan said the 330-acre campus will train an army of 14,000 new engineers a year, just for his company.

"For every employee, we have actually charted out a complete career plan—which takes them from a software engineer to potentially a CEO of the company," Gopalakrishnan said.

Freeman Hrabowski is president of the University of Maryland, Baltimore County. It's a small school that places a big emphasis on science, math and engineering.

"Clearly the more people we have who are prepared in those disciplines, the more inventors we'll have, the more people will be thinking about tech commercialization and starting jobs and starting new companies," he said.

Hrabowski is even sending his grad students into grade schools.

In just 10 years, sixth graders will be entering the labor market. But will the jobs be there for them?

America has done it before, made the investment in innovation and education that paid off in decades of unsurpassed prosperity.

"We have to start a lot of things. Not all of them are gonna work out," Rattner said. "In fact, only a tiny fraction of them will turn into an Intel or a Google or a General Electric. But if you're not investing, you're not giving yourself really a chance to play."

The benefits of those investments are often unexpected. But a ripple can grow into a wave, and that's how new industries and new jobs are born.

Changes to U.S. Economic and Tax Policies Would Add Millions of Jobs

Ross DeVol and Perry Wong

Ross DeVol is executive director of economic research at the Milken Institute, an independent economic think tank. Perry Wong is the director of regional economics at the Milken Institute.

The U.S. economy appears to be emerging from recession, but the severity of this downturn has left substantial underutilized resources in labor and product markets. To close the gap between actual and potential GDP [gross domestic product, a measure of a country's total economic output] as quickly as possible, economic growth must accelerate beyond current expectations. Unless sustainable growth is achieved, the unemployment rate will remain close to 10 percent in the immediate future and a portion of the nation's manufacturing capacity will continue to sit idle.

Economic and tax policy changes, combined with targeted investment in infrastructure, could effectively stimulate the economy in the near term while positioning the nation for sustained higher economic growth over the medium and long term. Given the current economic environment, a government-backed infrastructure program should be considered as an insurance policy to prevent further layoffs, stimulate job growth, and help restore the confidence of the American labor force.

Improving Economic and Tax Policy

Globalization has forever changed the international competitive landscape. Cross-border transactions, from trade to foreign direct investment, are now the norm. Given these

Ross DeVol and Perry Wong, "Jobs for America," Milken Institute, January 2010. © 2010 Milken Institute. Reproduced by permission.

developments, the United States must re-evaluate its policies relative to other nations on a regular basis. With this objective in mind, the Milken Institute [an economic think tank] set out to evaluate the impact of changing certain economic and tax policies that currently impede the nation's ability to compete.

A lower corporate tax rate makes the United States a more attractive location for business investment.

Specifically, we analyzed the potential effect of changing U.S. corporate tax rates, expanding the R&D [research and development] tax credit, and modernizing controls on exports of commercially available products to a representative group of countries. While the response to altering these policies would not be immediate, economic growth would improve during the second year of their enactment. . . .

Corporate Income Tax Policy

International differences in corporate income tax rates are a factor when firms determine where to locate their corporate headquarters, R&D activities, production facilities, and distribution networks—and today, the U.S. corporate income tax rate is second-highest among nations belonging to the Organisation for Economic Co-operation and Development (OECD) [a group of thirty industrialized nations]. With that in mind, we ran a simulation in which the U.S. federal corporate income tax rate was cut by 13 percentage points to 22 percent, with the reduction being phased in over a five-year period. This new rate would match the current OECD average.

Our results show that a lower corporate tax rate makes the United States a more attractive location for business investment by filtering through a reduction in the user cost of capital. After a rate cut is implemented, existing productive capacity in the U.S. is initially more heavily utilized to fulfill domestic final demand and boost exports. In today's economic climate, there are few capacity constraints that would restrict production from rising to meet increased demand. The impacts on annual economic growth in 2010 are not as large as in subsequent years, as it would take time for businesses to adjust their investment and production plans.

The long-term impacts of reducing the corporate income tax rate include the following:

- Real GDP growth improves by 0.3 percentage point on an annual basis from 2011 to 2013, an average of 0.2 percentage point from 2014 through 2017, and 0.1 percentage point in 2018 and 2019, relative to a baseline projection without a change in tax policy.

- Real GDP is $375.5 billion, or 2.2 percent, above the baseline projection in 2019.

- Exports respond to the lower corporate tax rate. By 2019, real exports stand at $233.3 billion, or 7.8 percent, above the baseline projection.

- Real business fixed investment jumps 4.6 percent, or $102.4 billion, above the baseline scenario in 2019.

- Industrial production in the rate-cut scenario exceeds the baseline by 3.9 percent in 2019, while total employment increases by 2.13 million (1.4 percent) and manufacturing employment rises by 350,000 (2.7 percent).

R&D Tax Credit Simulation

Although the United States pioneered the R&D investment tax credit in 1981, most other advanced economies have implemented their own more aggressive versions of this policy. Based on OECD calculations, the United States ranks 17th among member nations on the effective rate of the R&D tax credit. Furthermore, the U.S. has kept the R&D tax credit "temporary" for 29 years (in fact, it was recently allowed to expire again on December 31, 2009) and has imposed restrictions on qualifying. Many other OECD countries appear to have created a more attractive landscape for innovation and sustainable growth.

We evaluated the economic impact of increasing the R&D tax credit by 25 percent and making it permanent. In this scenario, businesses increase their research and development spending, therefore creating new products and services; enhancing productivity growth; expanding investment in technology-intensive capital equipment; spurring greater exports, production, employment, and incomes; and boosting overall real GDP growth.

The expanded R&D tax credit scenario produces the following results:

- Real GDP growth improves by 0.2 percentage point on an annual basis from 2011 to 2013, and by 0.1 percentage point after 2013, relative to a baseline projection without a change in policy.

- After 10 years, real GDP is $206.3 billion, or 1.2 percent, above the baseline projection in 2019.

- Real business fixed investment rises 5.6 percent, or $124.6 billion, above the baseline scenario in 2019.

- Exports, especially technology-related goods and services, experience higher growth. By 2019, real exports stand at $63 billion (2.1 percent) above the baseline projection.

- Industrial production exceeds the baseline scenario by 4.4 percent in 2019. Total employment rises by 510,000 jobs (0.4 percent) above the baseline at its peak in 2017, and manufacturing employment jumps by 270,000 jobs (2.1 percent) above the baseline in 2019.

Modernization of Export Controls

Here we assess the possible economic impacts of modernizing export controls on commercially available technology products for a representative group of countries. Proponents of modernization argue that "many current controls (outside of narrowly defined military niches) aimed at protecting national security harm U.S. innovation and competitiveness in global markets, thereby reducing economic prosperity, which is an essential element of U.S. national security."

It is not in our best economic interest to preclude the export of technology products that are legally available from other advanced and NATO [North Atlantic Treaty Organization, a group of sixteen Euro-Atlantic countries] member nations. The logic is that if the United States will not supply the desired technology, some other country will. For example, some multilateral agreements on export controls afford member countries the latitude to exercise their own discretion; this sometimes undermines the intent of such trade agreements. Because purchasing nations are able to obtain this technology elsewhere, U.S. policy is not ultimately effective—it simply prevents American firms from accessing new markets.

We assume that a responsible modernization of export controls for certain goods and certain countries would narrow the gap between U.S. market share in these nations and its share in the total world market by 50 percent.

The results of the adjusted export control scenario include the following:

- Modernizing U.S. export controls would produce higher export growth in the future, particularly in the high-value-added areas in which the United States excels.

- The most rapid period of export growth (0.2 to 0.3 percentage point on an annual basis) relative to the baseline occurs from 2011 to 2016, based on a 2010 implementation. After that, export growth relative to that in the baseline moderates to 0.1 percentage point annually. Real exports are $56.6 billion (1.9 percent) higher than the baseline in 2019.

- Real GDP rises by $64.2 billion (0.4 percent) relative to the baseline projection in 2019.

- Real business fixed investment grows faster in the adjusted export control scenario than in the baseline scenario over the next decade. It stands $18.7 billion (0.8 percent) above the baseline in 2019.

- Industrial production exceeds the baseline by 1.5 percent in 2019, while total employment increases by 340,000 jobs (0.2 percent) and manufacturing employment rises by 160,000 jobs (1.2 percent).

Infrastructure Investment

Globalization has upended the way we think about America's place in the world. Even with an issue like infrastructure, which once was considered purely a domestic concern, we have to consider the implications for the nation's ability to compete on an international stage. It has become painfully apparent that U.S. infrastructure, once the envy of the world, is now strained and aging, while other nations are constructing bullet trains, cutting-edge broadband networks, public transit systems, modern ports, and energy delivery systems, while making significant investments in alternative energy.

Modernizing the nation's infrastructure represents an opportunity to create thousands of jobs and stimulate the economy in the near term. In assessing the need, the American Society of Civil Engineers estimates it would take $2.2 trillion over the next five years to fix all the nation's infrastructure issues, including a projected $549.5 billion for highway spending.

Given the current pressures on federal, state, and local budgets, governments' ability to finance ambitious infrastructure investments is limited. It will be necessary to examine alternative approaches to funding, including public-private partnerships.

With this backdrop, we set out to determine the potential effects of various infrastructure investments on the job market, choosing 10 projects for study. The selected projects are high-impact investments in both high-growth and traditional industries that provide high-paying jobs, offering solid potential for sustainable development. All 10 projects fall under the broad themes of public safety, competitive transportation, and energy security, all of which are crucial for the United States. . . .

Taken together, the proposed investments amount to $425.6 billion. Highway and transit projects account for just over half the total investment pool. Investments in broadband infrastructure and onshore and offshore oil exploration account for the next largest investment amounts. All the projects combined will create 3.4 million construction- and R&D-related jobs, which will generate an estimated $147 billion in earnings. Accounting for ripple effects across other sectors, the total impact will add up to 10.7 million jobs, $420.6 billion in earnings, and $1.4 trillion in output. Because these impacts will likely be spread across a three-year period, it is important to note that the average annual increase would be 3.5 million jobs and $468 billion in output.

Average output per employee stemming from the total impacts from all projects amounts to about $132,000. Output per employee in 2009 across all non-farm sectors was slightly more than $108,000. The additional output per employee generated through these infrastructure projects reflects the valuable nature of such activity, the quality of the jobs that would be generated, and the incremental wealth that would be created.

Average wages across these projects would amount to $43,000 annually—substantially more than the current average of $30,500 across all private, service-providing sectors.

In addition, for every dollar invested in these projects, an additional $2.30 would be generated across all sectors. For every $1 billion invested in these projects, slightly more than 25,000 jobs are created.

Because most of the investments would be injected directly into the construction industry, some of the direct impacts may be short-lived as the initial funding dries up. But the indirect impacts would provide other sectors with a tremendous boost. In fact, of the 3.5 million jobs created per year, 9.2 percent (or 327,100 of them) would be in manufacturing. Manufacturing, services, and trade, all of which support various construction activities, would have the opportunity to capitalize on the investments.

Our project-by-project analysis shows the following results:

- Highway and transit investment of $225 billion over three years creates 6.2 million jobs (roughly 2 million per year), along with $238.2 billion in earnings and $775.4 billion in output.

- Broadband infrastructure investment of $55 billion generates nearly 1.1 million jobs (349,300 per year), along with $43.9 billion in earnings and $158.3 billion in output.

- Investment in offshore drilling and onshore exploration and development of oil and natural gas wells totaling $46.5 billion over three years creates 896,200 jobs (298,700 per year), along with $38.8 billion in earnings and $145 billion in output.

- Drinking water and wastewater infrastructure investment of $30 billion over three years results in 825,300 jobs (275,100 annually), along with $31.8 billion in earnings and $103.4 billion in output.

- Smart-grid investment of $24 billion over three years produces 649,600 jobs (216,500 annually), along with $25.1 billion in earnings and $82 billion in output.

- Nuclear energy investment of $15 billion over three years creates 397,300 jobs (132,400 annually), along with $15.6 billion in earnings and $48.7 billion in output.

- Renewable energy investment of $14.5 billion over three years generates 337,600 jobs (112,500 per year), along with $13.1 billion in earnings and $44.3 billion in output.

- Next Generation Air Transportation System (NextGen) investment of $10.4 billion over three years creates 181,900 jobs (60,600 per year), along with $8.9 billion in earnings and $32.1 billion in output.

- Inland waterway investment of $2.6 billion over three years generates 67,100 jobs (22,400 annually), along with $2.7 billion in earnings and $8.1 billion in output.

- Clean coal technology investment of $2.6 billion over three years creates 66,100 jobs (roughly 22,000 per year), along with $2.6 billion in earnings and $7.9 billion in output.

Boosting Entrepreneurship and Small Businesses Is Crucial to Job Creation

Mark Trumbull

Mark Trumbull is a reporter for the Christian Science Monitor *who focuses on business and the economy.*

If America is going to mount a solid recovery in jobs coming out of its deep recession, much of the fuel will come from people like Valentin Gapontsev, a Russian immigrant with a thick accent and a knack for turning beams of light into cash.

The company he heads isn't on the Fortune 500 list. It isn't located in a fancy mirror-skinned office building in downtown Boston. Instead, it resides down a blink-and-you'll-miss-it rural driveway, in a modest building where workers perform their tasks in white lab coats.

Yet the firm he founded, IPG Photonics, is putting this quiet community at the forefront of 21st-century laser technology. A decade after the IPG facility opened its doors in Oxford, Mass., nearly 400 people are now employed making equipment that manufacturers use for drilling, cutting, and welding metal parts—everything from car roofs to jet-engine combustors.

"Our target within 10 years is to triple our business, minimum," says Mr. Gapontsev, as he gazes from a conference room at the snow-gauzed woods outside.

One of a Kind?

Can you bottle what Valentin Gapontsev does? Is he one of a kind, or are there millions of Americans still out there whose

Mark Trumbull, "How America Can Create Jobs," *The Christian Science Monitor*, February 22, 2010. Reproduced by permission from *Christian Science Monitor*, (www.csmonitor.com).

skill, passion, and belief in the future [have] survived the worst battering since the bread lines of the 1930s?

Just saving American business from catastrophe was a heroic enough task over the past two years. Now, however, the focus has shifted to that one-syllable mantra that is the fundamental building block of economic growth: jobs.

Economists see firms like Gapontsev's—young, innovative, hungry—as crucial to job creation. What IPG Photonics does will have to be replicated exponentially across the country in everything from online start-ups to spade-in-the-ground food operations if the US is to put people back to work and raise living standards.

Innovative entrepreneurialism has always been at the core of America. It may now be the best hope for the return of the country's self-confidence or at the least, for simply putting Americans back to work.

The economy's net job losses over the past year have stemmed . . . from a sharp slowdown in the usual pace of new hiring—both by start-ups and long-established firms.

"We want companies that are going to double in size and growth in the next five years," says Elaine Allen, a professor of entrepreneurship at Babson College near Boston.

A Raft of Proposals

The idea isn't lost on President [Barack] Obama and other policy makers seeking an employment fix. The president has recently been selling a raft of proposals designed to boost both innovation and small-business job creation. Among them:

- A tax credit for new hiring this year [2010], with the benefits targeted especially toward small firms.

- Making the research and experimentation tax credit permanent, to become an $82 billion spur for innovation and investment this decade.

- Enlarging the pool of creative talent and skilled workers by revitalizing community colleges and making college loans more affordable.

Behind these moves lies a simple reality: The economy's net job losses over the past year have stemmed less from people losing their positions than from a sharp slowdown in the usual pace of new hiring—both by start-ups and long-established firms. During the recession, the number of jobs in the United States shrank by more than 8.4 million. The nation now has fewer private sector jobs than it did a decade ago, even though the population has grown by more than 20 million.

With that gaping jobs deficit, Mr. Obama's proposed incentives for bootstrap businesses are at best a partial fix. Many economists worry that the normal growth cycle may be too tepid to bring down the nation's 9.7 percent unemployment rate this year. So the president is pursuing more government aid to households and state governments, to give the economy a demand-side boost. He's also seeking to promote exports and to expand infrastructure spending.

Economists generally support this kind of multipronged strategy, but the basic goal is to get the economy's natural job-creation forces working again. The hiring will need to come from all quarters, including giant corporations and the hair salon down the street. Yet year in, year out, a healthy share of it comes from entrepreneurs, an American resource that dates back to Robert Fulton's steamboat.

So the questions loom: Where are the new Valentin Gapontsevs? How can America regain its entrepreneurial edge? Even more fundamentally, does the nation still have an innovative culture?

Tradition of Start-Ups

The encouraging news is that it does: America's tradition of garage-to-riches start-ups, extending from Alexander Graham Bell [inventor of the telephone] to Jeff Bezos [founder of Amazon.com], remains relatively vibrant. Successful entrepreneurs exist everywhere from the mountains of Montana to the glass-and-steel canyons of Chicago. Today they are more globally connected than start-up firms have ever been. They span every industry, not just high-tech fields like lasers. Many of the founders are immigrants, and their ranks are being expanded increasingly by women, minorities, and people over age 50.

Nor have the innovative ideas stopped flowing just because of a deep recession:

- In Kokomo, Ind., a city hit by the travails of the US auto industry, a new company called Zuna Infotech is hiring more than 100 people with computer skills. The firm is serving clients who want to outsource their information-technology work, but in this case the jobs will be "onshore" in the US rather than in cubicles in India.

- Across the southwestern US, Sprouts Farmers Market is turning home-grown cauliflower and navel oranges into big profits. Its concept—grocery stores that buy as much produce as possible from local farmers—has landed the Phoenix firm on *Inc.* magazine's list of fast-growing privately owned firms, yielding 2,500 jobs in just eight years.

- In the Boston area, a start-up called Pixily is growing jobs by helping small businesses ditch their file cabinets and store their documents digitally. Founder Prasad Thammineni, a serial entrepreneur from India, says he expects to double his payroll this year to about 20 employees.

"Being able to find information efficiently is the reason [businesses] find the service useful," says Mr. Thammineni.

Like many entrepreneurs, he stumbled on the idea for a business while trying to solve a problem—figuring out how to store his graduate-school notes. But what defines an entrepreneur is turning an epiphany into a viable product. In this case it took some nimble software, developed by a Pixily cofounder, that offers a no-fuss way to process all the documents that clients mail in monthly.

These kinds of employers represent the spearhead of job creation, even if many of them fail. "There's no question that they [high-growth firms] are critical to recovery," says Rob Atkinson, head of the Information Technology and Innovation Foundation, a think tank in Washington [D.C.]. "Their role in job creation is just so great."

Fascination with Entrepreneurs

The American fascination with entrepreneurs and inventors goes back at least to the days of Benjamin Franklin, the creator of bifocals and a wood stove. A confluence of forces contributed to the rise of a start-up culture. The young society blended egalitarian openness with acquisitive ambition. People had faith that they could achieve new things, but also a willingness to borrow ideas from an innovative Europe. The efforts fed on themselves as the nation developed a world-leading education system.

Firms in their first year account for about 3 in every 100 jobs at any given moment.

Despite its importance in American culture, the link between entrepreneurs and job creation is still only partially understood. Some analysts attribute the vast bulk of America's net job creation to start-up firms. But as vital as they are, it would be misleading to view them as the predominant source.

Modern economies are vast webs, where firms of all ages and sizes play important roles. Large firms, for example, often have the labs and know-how to be leaders in their fields. They usually provide better pay and benefits than smaller firms.

Still, firms in their first year account for about 3 in every 100 jobs at any given moment, according to recent research by the Census Bureau and the Kauffman Foundation. That's an enormous number—higher than the economy's net job creation in a typical year. Meanwhile, some of the start-ups that survive become big job creators as they aspire to be the next Facebook or FedEx.

Founts of Creativity

Newer companies matter for another reason. Although plenty of innovations emerge from research labs at übercorporations like IBM, entrepreneurial firms tend to be founts of creativity. Miles Flamenbaum, for example, is helping truck fleets do more with less on vehicle maintenance. He heads a company, SOMS Technologies, that sells "microGreen" oil filters that allow cars and trucks to go up to 30,000 miles without an oil change. It's a product that's environment friendly and can appeal during tough economic times.

"You can start saving [money] within that first 3,000 miles," says Mr. Flamenbaum, who launched the Valhalla, N.Y., firm in 2006 with the slogan: "Change your filter, not your oil."

True, innovation can lead to fewer jobs. If people are changing their oil less often, gas stations and Jiffy Lubes might have less business. Many new products marketed to US consumers are also as likely to create jobs overseas as in the US.

Still, the fact is, innovation usually leads to greater employment, not less. Someone, after all, has to staff the new oil filter business. Plus, as productivity and personal income rise as a result of innovation, consumers have more money to spend on other goods and services.

Innovation can create whole new industries, or enhance job opportunities within an industry. A quotidian example may be babysitting. Genevieve Thiers came up with the idea to found SitterCity, an online network to connect parents with sitters, as a college student. The year was 2001. Launching right after the dot-com bust (and as a music/English double major no less), she says she was "laughed out of the room" when she first sought start-up funds from investors.

After a bootstrap start, SitterCity has become a nationwide success. The firm currently employs 30 full-time people, with more on the way. But its bigger impact on the job market may be in home offices and high school lounges across the country. SitterCity's Web site now lists more than a million available caregivers, 45 percent of whom say they're now considering it as a career.

Ms. Thiers's service is essentially allowing people to create their own jobs: Her site now offers a gamut of home services, from elder and pet care to tutoring and babysitting.

Innovation can come in ways that benefit workers as much as consumers. Along the frothy Yellowstone River in Livingston, Mont., a business called PrintingForLess.com could also deserve the name "working for more." Providing an attractive office environment is integral to Andrew Field's recipe for print-shop success.

The company is known locally for its semicasual dress code, in-house day care, and dog-friendly policy inspired by Mr. Field's own border collie. These perks are matched by higher-than-average salaries, plus health care benefits. A person who works three 12-hour shifts a week can earn between $50,000 and $60,000 a year.

Huge Dividends

Field says this investment in keeping employees happy pays huge dividends by creating less turnover. That, coupled with his vision for reaching customers far beyond the northern Rockies with his online commercial printing operation, has spawned a robust business. The 14-year-old company has gone from 11 employees a decade ago to 130 today.

"We put a premium on high performance," says the denim-clad Field. "We tell our applicants that they shouldn't mistake the appearance of people walking around in boat shorts, flip-flops, and dogs lying at their sides with a casualness in execution. You need to be smart and motivated to work here."

So if start-ups are still starting and inventive minds are still inventing, what's the problem? In a word: money. Economists and businesspeople say it's one of the worst climates for entrepreneurs in decades. The slowdown in consumer spending is coupled with a credit crunch.

True, in official pronouncements, Washington authorities and some pundits suggest that the credit crisis has been easing over the past year. But don't tell that to John Joyce.

"I'm not seeing credit freeing up," says Mr. Joyce, who runs the Small BizNest, which helps young companies with marketing strategies. "The consensus is that this is the toughest [business climate] they've seen."

He sees the evidence right in the business park where he works in Shirley, Mass.: the printing firm that's profitable but was turned down for a loan to buy equipment; the painter whose American Express limit was cut back, removing a cushion that had helped him bridge gaps between revenues and payroll costs.

Some start-ups simply aren't getting started. Others are building their businesses more slowly than might otherwise be the case. In New York City, Vinicius Vacanti and Jim Moran are launching an e-mail-based service that sends consumers a customized bargain alert each week, tailored to their preferences for anything from stiletto heels to sit-down dinners. Launching in a recession, they aren't rolling in seed money for their firm, Yipit.com. "We practiced the lean start-up methodology," says Mr. Vacanti.

That means no employees right now (aside from one intern) and a focus on proving their business concept in just New York first. And they count themselves among the fortunate start-ups, having a friends-and-family network that has provided early funding.

Weak Environment Expected

Venture capital firms, in a recent survey, say they expect 2010 to be better for their industry than 2009 was. But that's not saying much. The survey, by the National Venture Capital Association, also found firms expecting a protracted weak environment.

"Venture capitalists will have to do more with less," Mark Heesen, president of the association, said in releasing the results in December.

Uncertainty about the policy landscape also poses challenges for new companies and small businesses. While proponents of the Obama administration's health care reforms argue that they will ultimately help the nation's economy, if passed, the bills would also impose new mandates on employers to pay for health coverage.

Another problem facing start-ups is the "brain drain" to other nations. America continues to educate and attract many highly skilled immigrants, who are among the most likely to help launch high-growth firms. But many others are now going elsewhere to study or returning home after attending college in the US.

Despite all the challenges, the US enjoys considerable strengths in its innovation economy. First, as the world's premier bastion of consumerism, there is no better place to give new products a try. Columbia University economist Amar

Bhide believes traditional theories of economic growth overestimate the role of scientific research and underestimate the role of "venturesome" consumers, people who take risks alongside the entrepreneurs by trying new products.

Second, businesspeople in America excel not just at technology but also on the "softer" side of innovation, the art of managing people. The success of Field's printing business in Montana doesn't stem simply from the confluence of the Internet and high-tech color presses. It's also his customer service, embodied in three-person teams that take each print job from start to finish.

Third, the US sports an array of supportive institutions, from university research labs to "incubator" business parks that offer low-cost office space and mentoring. Z Corporation, based near Boston, sprang up because the Massachusetts Institute of Technology (MIT) created technology for hitting a "print" button for three-dimensional objects.

If a 3-D printer sounds like something out of Willie Wonka's fantastical candy factory, just replace the confectioners' sugar with a less appetizing kind of white powder. The little granules get molded into any imaginable colorful shape—from prototypes of shoe soles to architectural models.

The challenge for the US, as it tries to recover from this recession and achieve longer-run prosperity, is to nurture . . . entrepreneurship.

"We've developed our own patent portfolio" since licensing the initial technology from MIT, says CEO John Kawola, whose 15-year-old firm now has 130 employees.

Many US start-ups are also increasingly "born global"— with blueprints that recognize customers might be in Sydney, Australia, and parts suppliers in Seoul, South Korea. Take IPG, the laser firm. As the company grows, new jobs could be added not just in the US but in the firm's Russian or German operations—or elsewhere. Gapontsev says his choice of locations hinges on two issues: finding top talent to hire and having access to key markets for his products.

His own Russian roots are a reminder that the US has never had any patent rights on ingenuity. As a scientist in Russia shortly after the Soviet Union collapsed, he became convinced that optical fiber could be the conduit for delivering much more laser energy than others believed to be feasible—and through a flexible cable ideal for computer-guided movements on the factory floor. Pursuing his vision, Gapontsev laid the groundwork for a company that has seen sales grow from $61 million in 2004 to $229 million in 2008, according to Deloitte, the accounting firm. "For America, there is only one way to compete with Asia," says Gapontsev—automate wherever possible.

It's clear that the rest of the world won't be standing still. The challenge for the US, as it tries to recover from this recession and achieve longer-run prosperity, is to nurture even more entrepreneurship. As Mr. Atkinson puts it: "We need the US economy to keep reinventing itself."

An Energy Efficiency Retrofit Program Could Add Many Construction Jobs

Bracken Hendricks and Matt Golden

Bracken Hendricks is a senior fellow with the Center for American Progress, a progressive think tank. Matt Golden is the founder and president of Recurve, a San Francisco company that provides home energy audits and energy remodeling/construction services to homeowners.

Today, 2.1 million construction workers are out of a job. Jobs are down 38 percent since 2006 in residential construction alone. This "tool belt recession" in the construction trades spills over to other parts of the economy as well. Because of declining demand for construction many manufacturing industry sectors that produce building products are currently operating at close to half their production capacity.

As devastating as these numbers are, however, the unemployment figures for construction are likely an understatement of the problem due to the large number of self-employed construction workers that do not show up in payroll statistics, so the jobs picture is even more urgent than even these data suggest. Further, more than 90 percent of contractors in the construction industry are small businesses—another hard-hit segment of the economy.

This [viewpoint] looks at data from the Census Bureau, the Federal Reserve, and the Bureau of Labor Statistics to demonstrate the urgent conditions facing blue-collar workers in America today and to show the capacity of the home performance retrofit industry to quickly scale in creating good American jobs in construction.

Bracken Hendricks and Matt Golden, "Taking on the Tool Belt Recession: Energy Efficiency Retrofits Can Provide a Real Help for Construction Unemployment," Center for American Progress, March 3, 2010. This material was created by the Center for American Progress. www.americanprogress.org.

This analysis clearly demonstrates that in addition to having an employment pool in construction that is ready to move quickly, the product manufacturers serving the industry have significant unused production capacity as well. So if demand for building products were to rise, U.S. manufacturers would quickly respond by putting laid off employees back to work.

Labor constitutes a very significant share of any remodeling job, but more than half of every dollar spent also flows to retail and manufacturing through product purchases. This means a program that incentivizes new construction investment through energy improvements would create jobs not only within the construction industry directly, but in retail, manufacturing, and other local economic activity as well.

Understanding the Tool Belt Recession

If you want to understand why Americans are uneasy about the future, take a look at what's happening to construction workers communities nationwide. While the U.S. unemployment rate finally dipped below 10 percent in January, construction industry unemployment actually jumped to 25 percent. If the economy as a whole, and the labor market in particular, is weak, for workers in the construction trades and the manufacturing and retail industries that support them, the situation is far more bleak.

The construction industry has suffered especially hard in this economic downturn, caught as it is in an economic vise between a financial crisis that has dried up lending for commercial real estate and the collapse of a housing bubble that has seen foreclosures skyrocket as housing prices fall.

Jobs in the construction sector and related industries are suffering more compared to other parts of the economy, resulting in sustained high unemployment and significant available manufacturing capacity. Consider the following:

Construction jobs

- The unemployment rate for experienced workers in construction was 24.7 percent in January 2010.

- Total construction payroll employment has dropped by 2.1 million jobs since 2006, with residential construction down by 1.3 million, or 38 percent.

- For 2009, 12.4 percent of all unemployed workers were previously employed in the construction industry.

- There have been 134,000 jobs lost (10 percent) in construction-related retail such as building supply stores and lumber yards since December 2007, with 186,000 lost (14 percent) since July 2006.

Manufacturing jobs

- Manufacturing employment has dropped 16 percent since the recession began, but the numbers are far worse in construction-related manufacturing, including:

  - Nearly 30 percent employment declines in wood products (148,000 jobs lost)

  - A close to 22 percent falloff in nonmetallic minerals jobs, such as window glass, gypsum products, and fiberglass insulation (107,000 jobs lost)

  - Nineteen percent of jobs in fabricated metals have disappeared, such as ductwork, metal windows, and doors (291,000 jobs lost), and 19 percent of jobs in HVAC [heating, ventilation, and air-conditioning] equipment as well (19,000 jobs lost)

- Overall "capacity utilization" in manufacturing—or the rate at which plants are operated compared to their potential—was 68.9 percent in December 2009. It was far worse for construction-related industries, with many operating at barely half their capacity, including wood products (51.5 percent), nonmetallic mineral products (54.0 percent), and fabricated metal products (63.9 percent)

- The vast majority of manufactured products and raw materials used in residential alterations and repairs are produced domestically, so the dollars spent on remodeling homes and buildings circulate primarily through the U.S. economy. In many categories of building materials the rate of domestic production is well over 90 percent. . . .

Forty-two of the 44 states with available data had seen job losses in excess of 10 percent of total construction jobs, 31 states had lost more than 20 percent of their construction jobs, 11 states had seen construction jobs drop by more than 30 percent, and four states had even seen a decline in construction employment of more than 40 percent of total jobs since the last peak in construction employment. In the seven states where reliable state-level numbers could not be determined, the overall trend of substantial job loss in construction, well above national averages for all industries, appeared to be very consistent.

This shocking drop in construction industry jobs, which we call the "tool belt recession," deserves specific attention and an urgent policy response. It is hard to foresee a robust economic recovery on the ground in communities when these near-depression-level conditions persist within local construction job markets.

Residential construction, including remodeling, typically declines before the overall economy enters a recession, and it experiences greater relative declines than other sectors. That has been especially true in the current episode. But investment in residential construction also tends to recover before the overall economy, leading the way out of recession. In the current recovery, however, residential investment's role as an engine of recovery has been missing.

Construction and construction-related industries have shed many jobs during this recession. From the national peak in the spring of 2006, payroll employment in residential construction declined from 3.45 million (seasonally adjusted) to 2.15 million, or nearly 38 percent. . . . Overall employment did not reach a peak until December 2007 and declined by 6 percent (from 138 million to 129.5 million). . . .

Some states show considerably higher construction job losses than the overall national decline of 26.2 percent. States particularly hard hit include California (−36.1 percent), Florida (−41 percent), Michigan (−42.6 percent), Arizona (−46.1 percent), and Nevada (−46.8 percent). California, Florida, and Texas shed more than 750,000 construction jobs combined since peak employment levels.

Employment in producing and distributing building materials also fell by more than overall employment in manufacturing and trade. Since December 2007, the total number of jobs in retail trade fell by 7.5 percent, but the decline during that period for building materials and garden supply stores was 10.4 percent. Employment in the wholesale trade sector, who supply those retail outlets, also declined by 22.5 percent for construction supplies compared to only 8.1 percent overall. The specific impact of job loss on industries connected to buildings and construction is undeniable and stands out starkly even in an otherwise weak national economic picture.

Because of the large self-employed construction workforce, the decline in jobs shown by the payroll statistics understates the total loss of jobs.

Similarly, manufacturing experienced widespread job losses, with an employment decline of 15.9 percent since December 2007. But construction-related manufacturing fell even more, with declines of 29.8 percent in wood products, 21.9 percent in nonmetallic minerals (including window glass, gypsum products, and fiberglass insulation), 18.7 percent in fabricated metals (ductwork, metal windows, and doors), and 19.3 percent in HVAC equipment.

Housing starts stabilized in recent months—at the lowest rate of production since World War II—but employment in residential construction and related industries continues to decline due to the lag between housing starts and completions. Moreover, growing weakness in nonresidential building construction of commercial buildings, and a growing financial crisis in commercial real estate, will likely continue to produce further employment declines in construction for some time to come.

Counting Job Loss for Self-Employed Construction Workers

Unfortunately, because of the large self-employed construction workforce, the decline in jobs shown by the payroll statistics understates the total loss of jobs. Economic Census data shows that the self-employed share of workers is significantly higher in the construction industry than in other sectors, at 16.6 percent in 2008.

The construction industry is highly fragmented and relies much more heavily on flexible labor markets than on capital equipment assets. This industry organization facilitates downsizing when demand falls but allows rapid expansion during recovery.

The industry includes general contractors, who organize complex projects and span a variety of functions, and special trade contractors, who perform specific types of work such as roofing or plumbing. Special trade contractors perform the vast majority of actual job-site production, whether for new construction or for alterations and repairs to existing structures. Many of these subcontractors are self-employed and tend to be undercounted in official job loss numbers.

General remodeling contractors, who direct work spanning several specialties, are more likely than new home builders to have construction workers as payroll employees, but even in remodeling, most production is subcontracted. Similarly, although some home centers and other retailers offer construction, installation, and home repair services, that work is also typically subcontracted.

Special trade contractors may be moderately large enterprises—with more employees than the general contractors they serve—but most are small businesses or self-employed independent contractors. For alterations and repairs to existing homes, the self-employed share is higher than the industry average because other construction segments such as bridge building have fewer self-employed workers.

Not all self-employed workers in the industry are individuals working on their own. Many are proprietors of unincorporated businesses with payroll employees. As a result, job loss data underreports the extent of the current jobs crisis and targeted efforts to help construction can have a very large ripple effect across local economies. . . .

Jump-Starting Demand for Manufacturing

There are currently large amounts of unused or underused capacity in labor markets and production facilities across America due to declines in both residential and nonresidential construction.

For instance, the unemployment rate for experienced construction workers was 24.7 percent in January 2010. Although that figure partly reflected seasonal factors, the average for 2009 was 19.1 percent, and the latest figure was 6.5 percentage points higher than in January 2009.

Lower capacity utilization rates translate into assembly lines that are lying idle, shifts that are not being worked, and large swaths of the workforce that have been furloughed or laid off. The overall capacity utilization rate in manufacturing was only 68.9 percent in December 2009 according to the Federal Reserve Board, meaning that nearly a third of our industrial capacity went unused. But it was even lower in some industries where we were putting barely half of our industrial capacity to use nationwide. This translates into rates of 51.5 percent for wood products, for example, 54.0 percent for non-metal mineral products, and 63.9 percent for fabricated metal products.

There are few areas where construction industry jobs seem poised to grow [except for] . . . the area of energy efficient retrofits of our nation's building[s].

The Federal Reserve monthly data on capacity utilization does not provide more detailed industry categories, but housing-related manufacturing is undoubtedly operating at even lower levels of capacity. Quarterly data with more detail from the Census Bureau show capacity utilization for paint, coatings, and adhesives at 56.7 percent in the third quarter of 2009 even though overall capacity utilization for the chemical industry group was around 72 percent.

What can be drawn from this data is that in addition to having an employment pool in construction that is ready to move quickly, the product manufacturers serving the industry have significant unused production capacity as well. If demand for building products were to rise, U.S. manufacturers would quickly respond by putting laid off employees back to work.

Building Demand for Jobs Through Home Energy Retrofits

Looking across the current economic landscape, there are few areas where construction industry jobs seem poised to grow.

There is one significant exception, however, in the area of energy efficient retrofits of our nation's building stock. A program that incentivizes energy improvements would rapidly create jobs within the construction industry directly, and in retail, manufacturing, and local economic activity as well.

Much of the improvement and repair costs for existing homes consist of labor and related costs performed on the job. But more than half of spending on home energy efficiency retrofits goes toward the cost of materials, distribution, and other purchased services. Of each dollar spent on alterations and repairs, about 9 percent goes directly to retail trade and about 3 percent to wholesale trade.

The share of residential remodeling, as well as other residential construction, that flows to and through retail trade is much larger than for other businesses, which may only obtain office supplies and other minor items through retail outlets. In part that reflects the uneven demands and fragmented structure of the industry. As a result, a construction crisis turns quickly not only into a crisis in manufacturing supply chains but becomes a crisis for retail and wholesale businesses as well.

Building materials retailers also provide services that go far beyond restocking shelves and ringing up purchases. Building materials retailers—including home centers, lumber yards, appliance dealers, hardware stores, and other specialty outlets—cut and fabricate products to specifications, deliver to job sites, handle special orders, track down obscure products and parts, and often extend credit. In other words, the impacts of a contraction in construction jobs deeply affect the broader local economy. But this also means that a program to expand demand for local construction jobs through retrofits would have far-reaching direct local benefits.

For state-of-the-art, high-energy-performance building components and mechanical systems—such as ultra-efficient heating, air-conditioning, and water heating equipment—as well as for insulated ducts and premium windows, the components represent a larger share of the installed cost. On-site labor, while not reduced, accounts for a smaller proportion of these jobs. Moreover, in the manufacture of such products, the amount of material used is greater than for standard-quality goods. For these areas of building retrofits, relative to weatherization activities such as air sealing, more employment would be created in manufacturing and in the supply chain rather than at the job site.

It is also worth noting that the vast majority of the manufactured products and raw materials used in residential alterations and repairs are produced domestically. This means construction industry jobs by their very nature disproportionately support American industries and workers.

Responding to the Tool Belt Recession with Retrofit Jobs

There are more than 2 million unemployed workers in construction and construction-related industries sitting on the sidelines in today's economy who need jobs that put their skills to use. The burgeoning home performance industry, which retrofits buildings to improve total energy efficiency and save consumers money, represents a massive and cost-effective opportunity to redeploy our nation's workforce and promote energy independence while addressing the need to cut energy bills, waste, and pollution.

The Center for American Progress [a progressive think tank] has estimated that cutting energy use by 20 to 40 percent in just 40 percent of America's building stock would create 625,000 sustained jobs over a decade and drive half a trillion dollars of new investment into the built environment, while saving as much as $64 billion every year on energy bills that consumers could spend in other ways. Retrofitting homes for efficiency is not just a matter of smart energy policy—it is also a bright spot in a weak economy where we can quickly jump-start investment to get contractors hiring again.

Smart public policy can help overcome current barriers to private investment in more energy-efficient buildings and jump-start jobs and growth in the construction trades and supporting industries. Currently, Congress is considering Home Star, a program of consumer incentives that provides a rebate to homeowners who invest directly in improving energy efficiency. Home Star would give homeowners a direct rebate when they buy a new efficient hot water heater, furnace, or air-conditioning system, and it could cut the cost nearly in half of replacing leaky windows, sealing ductwork, and insulating attics for millions of American homes. Building consumer demand for energy retrofits through Home Star will not only give consumers a rebate of as much as $3,000 to $8,000 and long-term savings on their energy bills, but it will create new demand for construction jobs, putting contractors back to work.

Home Star would be fast acting and use the existing marketplace to deliver retrofits to consumers with a minimum of new government overhead. It also builds a well-trained workforce and expands consumer demand for high-quality retrofits that provide guaranteed energy savings of 20 percent or more off existing energy bills. This is a policy that works rapidly to create urgently needed jobs today, even as it builds the robust industry that we will need for the future.

For maximum jobs benefits, federal policy should also target retrofits in commercial buildings through a Building Star program that increases investment in high-performance office buildings. These should likewise be matched incentives for industrial energy efficiency retrofits. A national strategy to reverse the tool belt recession should lead with a Home Star program for residential homeowners. There are other important job-creating policies under consideration today that would jump-start the market for energy-saving retrofits in both commercial and industrial buildings as well, and increase access to financing for retrofit jobs to speed the growth of these markets.

Current unemployment levels in the building and construction trades have reached crisis proportions. It is time for a national program to roll back these job losses and put hardworking Americans in the construction industry back on the job, rebuilding America for a clean-energy future that saves consumers money, improves health and comfort, and creates lasting value in our communities.

A Long-Term Economic Strategy Is Required to Create Good Jobs

Bob Burnett

Bob Burnett is a writer, an activist, and a Quaker from Berkeley, California.

While financial markets believe the great recession is over, millions of Americans continue to struggle. Unemployment is 10.2 percent and the more inclusive measure, underemployment, is at 17.5 percent. America's jobs crisis is both a short-term and long-term challenge.

A combination of circumstances brought us to this point. There's been a long-term decline in manufacturing jobs, which were replaced by employment in service industries: fathers who worked on Detroit's assembly lines making buses saw their jobs disappear and their sons and daughters employed driving buses. The US shifted from producing goods to providing services.

At the same time, we became more consumption oriented and less inclined to save. There was a fundamental shift in our values: Americans increasingly took a short-term perspective, went into debt to finance their lifestyle, and placed primacy on self-interest rather than the common good.

As the result of these trends and the meltdown in the financial services industry, by January 2009 the US economy was in terrible trouble. Many Americans were underemployed and deeply in debt. Furthermore, the US had lost its position as the world's preeminent economy; our competitiveness had been weakened by severe structural problems: health care costs, decaying infrastructure, energy costs, and an aging and undereducated workforce.

Bob Burnett, "Creating the Jobs America Needs," *The Huffington Post*, November 20, 2009. Reproduced by permission of the author.

Therefore, the [Barack] Obama administration faces both a tactical problem and a strategic challenge. Citizens need to have jobs as soon as possible but a sustainable recovery requires restructuring of the economy.

A Need for Long-Term Solutions

Several *short-term actions* have been proposed to reduce unemployment. One category requires further expenditure of federal funds. The initial stimulus package saved the jobs of millions of government workers—teachers, health care professionals, and first responders—by providing assistance to states and communities. As these entities continue to struggle, the scope of that rescue might be expanded. Furthermore, the first stimulus package provided $80.9 billion for infrastructure; creating a new infrastructure bank to finance big construction projects or expanding efforts to weatherize public buildings and homes could strengthen this effort. In addition, there could be New Deal–style employment programs such as the WPA [Works Progress Administration] and the CCC [Civilian Conversation Corps] [two work programs initiated during the 1930s Great Depression]. Given our jobs crisis, America might adopt the tactic that the federal government is our employer of last resort.

What's needed is a long-term economic strategy to ensure that America becomes more competitive in the global marketplace and, at the same time, generates high-quality jobs.

Another type of solution requires revised federal policies or tax laws. Economist Paul Krugman suggested the US should adopt policies that support private sector employment: "labor rules that discourage firing to financial incentives for companies that either add workers or reduce hours to avoid layoffs." The Economic Policy Institute proposed a new jobs tax credit "of 15% of expanded payroll costs in 2010 and 10% in 2011" that would create five million jobs. Economist Robert Reich argued that since big banks are not lending to small businesses, the US should "expand the Small Business Administration's [SBA's] lending programs and have the Fed [Federal Reserve] buy up the SBA's debt." There's been bipartisan support for a payroll tax holiday, as more than 80 percent of Americans pay more in taxes for Social Security and Medicare than they do in income taxes. Pending congressional legislation requires "small-business owners to invest the savings from the payroll tax holiday in hiring new workers or buying machinery or other investments to make their firms more productive."

Whether they involve increased federal funding or policy changes, these proposals are tactical; they treat all jobs as equal. However, creating new jobs at McDonald's is not the same as developing employment at a firm that produces wind turbines. Manufacturing jobs typically pay better than service sector jobs and, in the case of green jobs, have important social consequences.

What's needed is a *long-term economic strategy* to ensure that America becomes more competitive in the global marketplace and, at the same time, generates high-quality jobs. Some pundits want the federal government to pick winners, focus on certain industrial sectors. For example, they suggest Washington increase its investment in green jobs—manufacturing of electric cars—and deemphasize support for service industry jobs.

While there is wide support for government policies favoring green jobs, many progressives believe the US should adopt a more expansive industrial policy to address the structural problems besetting the US economy. The hope is that in the course of addressing problems such as education, energy, health care, and infrastructure the American marketplace will be stimulated: New opportunities will arise, creating high-quality jobs. Rather than have the Obama administration pick winners, a more expansive industrial policy would give entrepreneurs the opportunity to develop necessary new products and create meaningful jobs.

Obviously, short-term job-creation actions need to be taken, as well as remedial steps such as heightened regulations on financial markets. But the highest priority for the Obama administration is to articulate a national industrial policy to stimulate our entrepreneurial spirit, create meaningful jobs, and heighten our global competitiveness.

In 2010, the most important administration job-creation actions will be those that deal with the structural problems in the economy. The US needs to educate our citizens, provide them with affordable health care (and housing), change their energy habits and reduce their dependence upon fossil fuels, and bring America's decaying infrastructure into the 21st century. A new jobs initiative requires a strong foundation.

America Needs to Implement a Robust and Comprehensive Jobs Plan

Economic Policy Institute

The Economic Policy Institute is a nonpartisan think tank devoted to achieving a prosperous and fair economy.

Almost 16 million Americans are out of work. They are our husbands and wives. Our children, our parents. Our neighbors. The supply of willing workers is overwhelming, but we don't have the demand to match. Americans want to work. Putting the American people back to work is not only an economic imperative, but a moral one as well. Americans value hard work, independence, and personal responsibility. American workers are remarkably resilient and have an unrivaled work ethic. In the face of these challenging economic times, Americans who have jobs are working hard, gaining new skills, caring for their parents, and providing for their children. Americans who don't have jobs are doing everything they can to find work. Their quiet resilience has been a little-noticed source of our nation's strength and it can also be a wellspring for our nation's renewal.

The Current Situation

The United States is facing its worst unemployment crisis of the last 70 years. Nearly 16 million Americans are out of work, one-third of whom have been jobless for over six months. Another 9.3 million Americans are working part-time because they can't find the full-time jobs they want and need. The jobs shortage is so severe that there are now six

"American Jobs Plan: A Five-Point Plan to Stem the U.S. Jobs Crisis," Economic Policy Institute, December 2009. Reproduced by permission.

unemployed workers for every job vacancy—double the ratio in the prior recession of the early 2000s.

The nation [should] . . . strengthen the safety net . . .; provide fiscal relief to state and local governments; make renewed investments in transportation and schools; support direct creation of public service jobs; and establish a new job creation tax credit.

The American Recovery and Reinvestment Act passed earlier this year [2009] helped to pull the economy out of its nosedive and to dampen mounting job losses. Still, the jobs crisis has persisted, and it is likely that unemployment will remain above 8% *even two years from now* in the absence of bold and decisive action to create jobs. The employment situation is an economic and moral crisis for the nation and requires an adequate, comprehensive response by the federal government. By itself, the private sector is unable to create jobs in the numbers the United States needs for a robust, full economic recovery.

The Economic Policy Institute recommends a five-point American Jobs Plan to create jobs and stem the unemployment crisis. The plan calls for the nation to strengthen the safety net (including unemployment compensation, COBRA [Consolidated Omnibus Budget Reconciliation Act, a law that gives fired or laid-off workers the right to continue group health benefits] health coverage, and nutrition assistance); provide fiscal relief to state and local governments; make renewed investments in transportation and schools; support direct creation of public service jobs; and establish a new job creation tax credit.

The American Jobs Plan is an efficient and effective way to create jobs. We estimate that the plan will create at least 4.6 million jobs in the first year, at a total first-year *gross* cost of roughly $400 billion. This entire cost can be recouped within

10 years by enacting a financial transactions tax (FTT), which would take effect three years after enactment. An FTT is a highly progressive way to raise revenue by imposing a small tax on the sale of stocks and other financial products.

Jobs Created by the American Jobs Plan

Each of the five points of the American Jobs Plan would have a significant impact on job creation. . . .

Safety net spending. The investments in safety net programs (unemployment insurance and COBRA) would create jobs indirectly because those receiving assistance will have greater disposable income to spend on goods and services. An additional $110 billion in these programs would increase nationwide employment by 931,000 jobs.

Relief to state and local governments. Fiscal relief to state and local governments would prevent many public sector layoffs and create jobs in the private sector. States are currently facing several budget crises. For fiscal year 2011 (which starts in July 2010), state and local governments are facing a $182 billion shortfall, even after including $38 billion in Recovery Act [the American Recovery and Reinvestment Act] assistance for that year. Without assistance, they will be forced to fire public sector employees (such as teachers and first responders), cut programs, raise taxes, or some combination of the three. All of these adjustments would also harm private sector employment, since the reduction in disposable income for those laid off would lead to less consumption of goods and services. Private sector employment would be further harmed as private firms that directly deliver services based on state funding—organizations such as hospitals, nursing homes, and construction contractors—are forced to cut back as well. Additional assistance of $150 billion to state and local governments would increase employment by about one million jobs. About half of this employment impact would be in the private sector.

Investments in schools and transportation. The Recovery Act contained additional funding for the nation's infrastructure, including roads, bridges, and waterways. However, one element that was initially included but then stripped out of the final version was money for improvements to school buildings. Adding $30 billion to restore school facility funding and adding to other infrastructure investments would boost employment by 239,000 jobs.

These three components of the American Jobs Plan—each of which is an extension or augmentation of the Recovery Act—would in total boost employment by 2.2 million jobs. However, given the severity of the downturn, we must also look to new policy to spur employment in the private sector and to employ people directly to provide public services.

Public service jobs. The United States has a long history of direct public service employment in times of economic crisis, and a new program today could be targeted at distressed, high-unemployment communities and provide services such as environmental cleanup, community policing, before- and after-school care of children, demolition or boarding up of abandoned houses and buildings, and parks improvements. A $40 billion investment in public service employment would employ an estimated 1 million people.

Job creation tax credit. The job creation tax credit would provide a temporary credit to firms that expand employment. The approach would give businesses a credit of 15% of expanded payroll costs in 2010 and 10% in 2011. The credit could spur an estimated 1.4 to 2.8 million new jobs in 2010 and 1.1 to 2.3 million in 2011.

Taken together, the gross cost of the five components of the American Jobs Plan is roughly $400 billion in the first year. However, the *net* cost of the plan would be much lower; we estimate that roughly 40 cents of each dollar spent on the plan would be recouped through higher revenue induced by increased economic activity, as well as reduced spending on existing safety net programs.

In total, the extension and augmentation of the Recovery Act together with the public service employment proposal would add about 3.2 million jobs to the economy that would otherwise not exist. A final estimate of the American Jobs Plan is more difficult because of how the tax credit might interact with other aspects of the jobs proposals; however, a conservative estimate would suggest that the total package, using the lower bound estimate of the job-creation tax credit, would lead to at least an additional 4.6 million jobs over the first year.

The Need for Bold Action

To help the tens of millions of Americans who are unemployed or underemployed, Congress and the [Barack] Obama administration should take bold, decisive action to create jobs. The Recovery Act passed earlier this year helped pull the economy out of its sharp descent. But the American people, who see unemployment as one of the most important economic problems facing the country, overwhelmingly favor additional action to create jobs. The American Jobs Plan would create at least 4.6 million jobs in the first year alone. Over a 10-year period, the entire cost of the plan would be paid for with a financial transactions tax.

Organizations to Contact

Apollo Alliance
330 Townsend Street, Suite 205, San Francisco, CA 94107
(415) 371-1700 • fax: (415) 371-1707
Web site: www.apolloalliance.org

The Apollo Alliance is a coalition of labor, business, environmental, and community leaders working to catalyze a clean energy revolution to put millions of Americans to work in a new generation of high-quality, green-collar jobs. Inspired by the Apollo space program, the group promotes investments in energy efficiency, clean power, mass transit, next-generation vehicles, and emerging technology as well as in education and training. The Apollo Alliance's Web site contains a section on green jobs and is a source of various articles and publications, including *Clean Energy Corps* and *Winning the Race: How America Can Lead the Global Clean Energy Economy*.

Cato Institute
1000 Massachusetts Avenue NW,
Washington, DC 20001-5403
(202) 842-0200 • fax: (202) 842-3490
Web site: www.cato.org

The Cato Institute is a libertarian public policy research foundation headquartered in Washington, D.C. The institute is named for *Cato's Letters*, a series of libertarian pamphlets that helped lay the philosophical foundation for the American Revolution. Cato's mission is to promote public policies based on the principles of limited government, free markets, individual liberty, and peace. The group publishes a variety of publications, including books, monographs, briefing papers, and studies; a quarterly magazine, *Regulation*; and a bimonthly newsletter, *Cato Policy Report*. The Cato Institute's Web site includes a list of publications relating to the recession and the need to create jobs. Examples include *Only Real Reform Will Resolve Crisis* and *The Fallacy of Economic Security.*

Center for American Progress (CAP)
1333 H Street NW, 10th Floor, Washington, DC   20005
(202) 682-1611 • fax: (202) 682-1867
Web site: www.americanprogress.org

The Center for American Progress (CAP) is a progressive think tank that works on present-day challenges such as energy, national security, economic growth and opportunity, immigration, education, and health care. CAP develops new policy ideas, critiques the policies that stem from conservative values, and challenges the media to cover the issues that truly matter. The group also produces numerous reports and policy papers addressing job and economic issues. Recent publications include *A Woman's Nation Changes Everything* and *Green Recovery: Building a Low-Carbon Economy.*

Economic Policy Institute (EPI)
1333 H Street NW, Suite 300, East Tower,
Washington, DC   20005-4707
(202) 775-8810 • fax: (202) 775-0819
e-mail: researchdept@epi.org
Web site: www.epi.org

The Economic Policy Institute (EPI) is a nonprofit think tank dedicated to improving the economic condition of low- and middle-income American workers. EPI conducts research on the status of American workers and provides economic information to policy makers and the public. It issues a biannual report titled *State of Working America,* which provides a comprehensive analysis of the U.S. labor market and is available on its Web site. EPI's Web site is also the source of numerous other publications, reports, and news about the U.S. economy.

New America Foundation
1899 L Street NW, Suite 400, Washington, DC   20036
(202) 986-2700 • fax: (202) 986-3696
Web site: www.newamerica.net/

The New America Foundation is a nonprofit, nonpartisan public policy institute focused on issues involving the changing conditions and problems of the current information-age economy—an era shaped not only by transforming innovation and wealth creation but also by shortened job tenures, longer life spans, mobile capital, financial imbalances, and rising inequality. The foundation's Web site contains numerous articles, blogs, and policy reports relevant to the jobs crisis, the economy, and America's future, including a recent policy paper titled *The Jobs Deficit: The Challenge of Putting Americans Back to Work.*

Surdna Foundation

330 Madison Avenue, 30th Floor, New York, NY   10017
(212) 557-0010
Web site: www.surdna.org

The Surdna Foundation seeks to foster just and sustainable communities in the United States—communities guided by principles of social justice and distinguished by healthy environments, strong local economies, and thriving cultures. The foundation awards grants in the United States in the areas of sustainable environments, strong local economies, and thriving cultures. The group also publishes an annual report and offers commissioned reports on a range of topics, including for example, *Economic Development and Workforce Development Systems: A Briefing Paper.*

U.S. Bureau of Labor Statistics

2 Massachusetts Avenue NE, Washington, DC   20212-0001
(202) 691-5200
Web site: www.bls.gov

The U.S. Bureau of Labor Statistics (BLS) is the principal fact-finding agency for the federal government in the broad field of labor economics and statistics. The agency collects, processes, and analyzes statistics on hours of work, average hourly earnings, employment and unemployment, consumer prices, and other economic matters. BLS is an official source of information for data such as the national unemployment rate, state unemployment rates, inflation levels, employment projections, and similar job-related issues.

Bibliography

Books

Christopher M. Davis, David Obey, and TheCapitol.Net	*Economic Policy Crisis and the Stimulus: Analyses of the American Recovery and Reinvestment Act (ARRA) of 2009 HR 1, 111th Congress.* Alexandria, VA: TheCapitol.Net, Inc. 2009.
Lynne A. Dunbrack	*The Economic Stimulus Bill: A "HITECH HIT."* Framingham, MA: IDC, 2009.
Francis Green	*Demanding Work: The Paradox of Job Quality in the Affluent Economy.* Princeton, NJ: Princeton University Press, 2007.
Van Jones	*The Green-Collar Economy: How One Solution Can Fix Our Two Biggest Problems.* New York: HarperOne, 2008.
Todd A. Knoop	*Recessions and Depressions: Understanding Business Cycles.* Santa Barbara, CA: Praeger 2010.
Les Leopold	*The Looting of America: How Wall Street's Game of Fantasy Finance Destroyed Our Jobs, Pensions, and Prosperity, and What We Can Do About It.* White River Junction, VT: Chelsea Green Publishing, 2009.

| Joel Makower | *Strategies for the Green Economy: Opportunities and Challenges in the New World of Business.* New York: McGraw-Hill 2009. |

| Andrew P. Morriss et al. | *7 Myths About Green Jobs.* Bozeman, MT: PERC, 2009. |

| Organisation for Economic Co-operation and Development (OECD) | *OECD Employment Outlook 2009: Tackling the Jobs Crisis.* France: OECD Publishing, 2009. |

| Jack Rasmus | *Epic Recession: Prelude to Global Depression.* London: Pluto Press, 2010. |

| David Rhodes and Daniel Stelter | *Accelerating Out of the Great Recession: How to Win in a Slow-Growth Economy.* New York: McGraw-Hill 2010. |

| Jerry Martin Rosenberg | *The Concise Encyclopedia of the Great Recession 2007–2010: Meltdown.* Lanham, MD: Scarecrow Press, 2010. |

| Jack Stone and Joe McCraw | *Unemployment: The Shocking Truth of Its Causes, Its Outrageous Consequences and What Can Be Done About It.* Victoria, BC, Canada: Trafford Publishing, 2007. |

| Michael Heng Siam-Heng | *The Great Recession: History, Ideology, Hubris and Nemesis.* London: World Scientific Publishing Company, 2010. |

Dan Sinas   *Job Killers: How Governments'
                          Increasing Role in the Workplace
                          Reduces Profits and Increases
                          Unemployment . . . and the Solution
                          . . . Get Americans Back to Work Now.*
                          Bloomington, IN: iUniverse, 2010.

Samuel P. Turner,   *Economic Stimulus: Plans, Risks and
ed.   Outlook.* Hauppauge, NY: Nova
                          Science Publishers, 2009.

Periodicals

Jeannine Aversa   "Jobs Crisis Seems to Ease:
                          Unemployment Holds Steady,
                          Employers Make Fewer Cuts than
                          Expected," *Business News*, March 5,
                          2010. http://blog.taragana.com.

Steve Benen   "Breakthrough Month for the Job
                          Market . . . ," *Washington Monthly*,
                          April 2, 2010.
                          www.washingtonmonthly.com.

Rich Blake and   "Ten Ways to Create Jobs and Put
Alice Gomstyn   America Back to Work as
                          Unemployment Rate Drops to 10%,"
                          ABC News, December 4, 2009.
                          http://abcnews.go.com.

Josh Dorfman   "How to Sell Green Jobs to America,"
                          Huffington Post, March 25, 2010.
                          www.huffingtonpost.com.

Kelly Evans   "Jobless Rate Tops 8%, Highest in 26
                          Years," *Wall Street Journal*, March 7,
                          2009. http://online.wsj.com.

Rana Foroohar   "Growing Green Jobs: Beware
                   Politicians Promising to Put Millions
                   to Work in a New 'Green Economy.'
                   They Can't Deliver," *Newsweek*,
                   March 29, 2010. www.newsweek.com.

Justin Fox   "Will Obama's Stimulus Package
                   Work?" *Time*, January 9, 2009.
                   www.time.com.

Thomas L.   "Green the Bailout," *New York Times*,
Friedman   September 27, 2008.
                   www.nytimes.com.

Heather Green   "Green Jobs and the Future,"
                   BusinessWeek, February 27, 2008.
                   www.businessweek.com.

Emily Kaiser   "Will the U.S. Job Market Break Its
                   Losing Streak?" Reuters, January 3,
                   2010. www.reuters.com.

Paul Krugman   "Free to Lose," *New York Times*,
                   November 12, 2009.
                   www.nytimes.com.

David Leonhardt   "Judging Stimulus by Job Data
                   Reveals Success," *New York Times*,
                   February 16, 2010.
                   www.nytimes.com.

Ryan McCarthy   "'No Labor Market Recession for
                   America's Affluent,' Low-Wage
                   Workers Hit Hardest: STUDY,"
                   Huffington Post, February 10, 2010.
                   www.huffingtonpost.com.

Catherine
Rampell
"The Growing Underclass: Jobs Gone Forever," *New York Times*, January 28, 2010. http://economix.blogs.nytimes.com.

Jerome Ringo
"Green-Collar Jobs—the Future of the Global Workplace," *Scientific American*, December 2008. www.scientificamerican.com.

Steve Selengut
"How to Create More Jobs, America," *Fortune Watch*, September 9, 2009. www.fortunewatch.com.

Wall Street Journal
"Best and Worst Jobs 2010," January 5, 2010. http://online.wsj.com.

Bryan Walsh
"What Is a Green-Collar Job, Exactly?" *Time*, May 26, 2008. www.time.com.

Tara Weiss
"The 10 Hardest Jobs to Fill in America," Forbes.com, June 3, 2009. www.forbes.com.

Index